MW01612532

# Jimmy the Greek

## *American Citizen*

Jmmy

PROIOS

## Jimmy Proios

To April

Prepared for publication by:

www.40DayPublishing.com

Cover design by Jonna Feavel

www.40DayGraphics.com

Printed in the United States of America

# Acknowledgements

I am so thankful for this great country I live in, the country I raised my family in, the country I am proud to be a citizen of: The United States of America.

I am also grateful for my granddaughter, Alexandra and my grandson, Soto, without whom this book would never have happened. Thank you to my children, Peter and Sophia, for your commitment to our family and sticking close. Family is everything.

I also want to thank my lovely bride, Stella. We are blessed. We have been through hard times and good times, ups and downs. We'll always remember where we came from and perhaps through the pages of this book, our great grandchildren will also know where they came from.

To all the rest of my family, both living and passed, I am thankful. Again, family is everything.

# Foreword

For as long as I can remember my grandfather was always remembering a story or an experience that happened to him. He was filled with many and I love to hear them all. A boy on an island caught between a war, a journey to America, working and running restaurants, joining the US Navy, moving across the US to start multiple businesses,

When I was younger I didn't pay much attentions to the stories or appreciate them as much. But as I got older it was very interested and I started to sit down and listen. He would tell me. I would like to write a book someday. He had mentions this more than once, and I always thought it would be a great idea. For someone to travel across the world during a war, and start a new life in America, which he gave me the privilege to be able to help him do such a thing tells me its worth for his story to be heard and one to forever live in our bloodline. Also, it personally gives me reference to go back and reread since we can't remember all the details or a story.

He means the world to me and inspires me a lot, a man who has taken the negative and turned it into positivity and kept on trucking. Also, a man that literally loves life. I've never seen someone so happy on a Monday, Tuesday, Wednesday, Thursday, Friday, Saturday, or Sunday. It does not matter the day, the week, the month, or situation. He is always there with a smile and ready for that experience. I've never heard him say I cannot, I've never seen him take an easy route, I've Never seen him slack. in his 80s still at work every day walking, communicating and keeping up with today's technology it amazes me.

I am still able to learn from him till this day and I am very thankful for that. My Father passed at an early age, and I was young myself, so I looked up to my grandfather for guidance and this is an honor for me to help write a book for him. I hope you all enjoy these stories and experiences as much as I did.

-Soto Gardias

# Chapter 1
# Life After Death

*"Excess of grief for the dead is madness; for it is an injury to the living, and the dead know it not." Xenophon, Historian of the 4th century BC*

I was born on July 9, 1937 on Leros, a Greek island in the southern Aegean Sea, and then I died. No really, I died. I would not lie to you. I suppose this would be a very short book if the story stopped here. Lucky for you, there is life after death. I have a good memory, but not that good. So, I'll tell you the story as it was told to me.

I was six months old when my mother became concerned. I was drinking plenty of milk, but nothing was coming out the other end. What can I say? I liked food. I still do. She told her friends about my dilemma who assured her some babies use everything they take in. I must have needed more than the average baby because, well, let's face it, my mother had a superior baby. So, eh…that's how it happens sometimes. My mother accepted this explanation. Who was she to argue? Besides, she already knew I was an exceptional baby.

Unfortunately, I became bloated and my heart quit beating. Exceptional or not, I was dead. Too much in. Too little out. I was my mother's fourth child but apparently, I was the only one who had this issue and I was certainly the only child to die and come back to life. Have you ever attended a Greek funeral? Let me tell you about one. Well, to be specific, mine.

There are four parts to a traditional Greek funeral. Part one is the disposition. Basically, I was wrapped in a blanket and placed on the middle of the table for a 24-hour wake. Mourners, all women dressed in black, were gathered around the table crying and screaming. Some were pulling out their hair. Some were ripping their clothing. All were appropriately demonstrating their grief, as was expected on our little island.

A small casket near the table served as a practical method to carry a body to the gravesite. Once at the gravesite, however, the body was removed from the casket and placed in the ground. The casket was then stored and used for the next baby who died.

When the appropriate amount of wailing had taken place, one of the women started to pick me up to put me in the casket for the procession to the cemetery. Startled, she put me right back on the table and looked at my mother. "Sophia, this baby is not cold. He's hot!"

They quickly called for what passed for a doctor on the island. He tapped my belly. "This baby is full!" He didn't have a stethoscope, so he put his ear on my chest.

He heard gurgling. He held my wrist and felt for a pulse. "This baby isn't dead. He's so full of his mama's milk, he can't move. This child needs an enema!"

The good news was the last three parts to a Greek funeral, the transportation of the body, the planting of grave flowers and the dinner for the mourners, were thankfully, completely lost on me. Perhaps the dinner for the mourners turned into a celebratory dinner.

When the mourners return to the home of the deceased, they steal something from the house. It's a tradition. They become scavengers and just take something they want. Believe it or not, it's not even to remember the deceased by. It's just because the family has something they want. I know, we're strange. It's possible this practice came from the ancient Greek practice having to do with vases and the dead. Vases seemed to have a particularly important role in the death of a man, specifically as a monument to the dead person and as a vessel for the spirit of the dead. This is just one theory, but, the thieving could have come from the practice of stealing the vases. Someone, somewhere along the line, changed the rules from stealing a vase to stealing anything you might want...perhaps a person's shoes? Perhaps a picture from the wall. Or maybe, the mourner coveted the person's lamp. If the origin didn't come from the vases, I have no idea where that practice came into play. Since I came back to life I'm guessing this part of the traditional funeral was skipped as well. Then again, who knows. We're Greek. Anything can be explained away. My mother would have been busy with a baby who had an enema, so it's possible a few days later she was searching endlessly for her broom! I'm sure she didn't care! Her baby was alive!

A few years later, when I was a young boy, I would help the priests at church. There was a custom, since the bodies were not buried in a casket in the ground and since the island was only so big and the gravesites only so many, after a period of three years, the bones of the decomposed bodies would be dug up and returned to the deceased's families. The gravesites could then be used by someone else—similar to reusing the casket. The priests would accompany the grave diggers to pray over the bones being retrieved from their temporary resting place. Because I wanted to be a priest when I grew up, I would accompany the priests to the gravesites. There were instances when the graves were dug up and the bones were not in the original position as when buried. Some were facing the wrong direction. Some had turned around and where the feet were supposed to be, the skull rested. All this indicated some people were buried alive. The thought made me shudder just a bit. That could have been me. Thinking about it still gives me the creeps. Later they started adding cords that a person could pull which, when pulled, would ring bells to attract attention in case a person was accidently buried alive. Could you imagine? Yeah, me either.

I'm getting ahead of myself. We should be introduced. I was born Dimitrious Proios, after my grandfather on my mother's side. My children call me pop. My grandchildren call me pops or Pappous (Greek for Grandfather) when they were little. My wife, Stella calls me…never mind. She'll get embarrassed. You, you can call me Jimmy. I'll tell you all about my American name later.

Once I got past almost being buried alive, the first few years of my life were great. In fact, my father was a wealthy man and we lived a rather comfortable life. We may not have had running water or electricity—no one on Leros had those—but we always had a roof over our heads and food for ourselves and those around us. Not many on the island could boast about that. There were hard times and we helped each other—which is how Greeks lived.

Because my father was a wealthy man, I was one of the few babies who had a carriage to ride around in. When I got older I would chase the cat down and use the carriage to give him rides. He got so used to riding in the carriage, he would see me coming and jump in himself. I would like to think I have that much influence, but I'm thinking the cat was just a smart, trainable cat!

In Leros, my father was known as Pablo. Later, after traveling to and becoming an American citizen, he was known as Paul. On Leros he owned a tavern, basically a restaurant, coffee shop, bar and general hub all rolled into one for those in the community. If someone was hungry, and they had no money or nothing to trade, my father would give them and their family a meal and write it down as an IOU. Most of the time he never received any type of payment. That was the kind of man my father was. He was compassionate.

He was also an entrepreneur. He made wine from grapes he imported from other islands. He also made

Ouzo, a strong drink still popular in Greece today. On the back of the tavern was a small addition my father used for manufacturing cigarettes. He employed locals to roll them and he would sell them for profit. He diversified before diversifying was a thing. On Leros, before the war, he was a smart businessman.

After hours the back room became a place for men to gather to play cards and gamble. My father didn't run the gambling, but he did take a profit for allowing the men to use his tavern—he rented the room out. He also acted as a bouncer of sorts. Many times, he'd have to toss a sore loser out the door. His philosophy was, you knew what you were getting into before you began playing cards. Don't come crying when you lose all your money. You should have thought of that before you started gambling. Not everyone thought the way he did. Especially those who lost all their money. He wasn't mafia, but some of that Italian influence may have rubbed off on him. He was tough, but fair.

My father may have been a powerful figure in our community, but my mother, Sophia, was the one who held everything together in our home and in my father's business, specifically the tavern. She was the glue of our family. She was my mountain. The one I looked up to. She did all the cooking, both in the tavern as well as upstairs where we lived. She served. She cleaned. She did the shopping. She washed the clothes. She chased us down and made sure we got to school. She did everything but enter the town square. That, she did not do. Then again, during that time no women entered the square. That was the men's domain. There wasn't much else my mother didn't do. My sisters and brothers and I would hang on her apron strings as she worked. She made spaghetti in very large pots that were often used for dirty laundry. Spaghetti you ask? On a Greek island? Yes. Spaghetti.

As I mentioned before, the first three and a half to four years of my life were lived in comfort. Not only were my physical needs provided by hard working, loving parents, but I lived on paradise. Literally.

Leros is just one island of a group of islands called, Dodecanese Islands—meaning 12 islands—in the Aegean Sea. In Greek Mythology, it was believed Leros was protected by the goddess, Artemis, because she protected the high deer population the island once boasted.

The island itself is a little over 9 miles long and just under 21 square miles in total. At her narrowest point, Leros is just over nine tenths of a mile. Meaning, you can stand between the two shores and see ocean to the right and to the left. There are cliffs and bluffs, pine trees, eucalyptus trees, and olive trees. There are beaches and even mountains. Beauty, everywhere you look. How much beauty can one person take? For some, they can view beauty their entire lives. Others can only stand so much.

It wasn't her beauty though that made Leros attractive to the English, the Germans, the Turks and the Italians among many more throughout history. It was the many inlets that proved to be, as described by some, the best natural harbors in the Mediterranean. In fact, Lakki, is the deepest harbor in all the Mediterranean.

There was a 400-year period which Leros was not part of Greece. From 1829 until 1912, the Turks ruled on Leros. On May 12, 1912, Italy, in a war with the Turks, seized the island of Leros. The Italians controlled the island for 31 years. And you wonder why we ate spaghetti on a Greek island? There is your answer. It is rumored the Turks still want Leros and are making plans to take her back. They are flying over the island and claim the flights are just exercises—maneuvers, but, I wouldn't put anything past them. Then again, Leros is about 30 miles from the coast of Turkey and 230 miles from Athens. I suppose it would be hard for a Turk plane not to fly over Leros.

For 31 years the Italians worked to improve living on the island of Leros, especially in the city of Lakki. Greek schools taught Italian as the primary language. The Italians, intent on strengthening their navy, started the task of modernizing Lakki, beginning with a naval base. In fact, it is rumored that Mussolini himself loved the island of Leros and had a mansion in Lakki.

There is a story, I'm a little sketchy on all the details, but, it was told to me and I will pass it on to you. Mussolini, in one of his treks around the island, stopped at my father's tavern for something to drink. Soldiers surrounded our tavern and he came in looking for refreshment. I was small, just a little boy, and had been learning the song, Mamma, in school. It was written in 1940 and became famous worldwide, including in the United States. He saw me playing in the tavern, so he pulled me up on his knee. To his great delight, at my parent's encouragement, I sang the song Mamma. Mussolini wanted all the children on the island to learn Italian, so he made us take it in school therefore I learned the song in Italian. This made him very happy.

My father was an easy going resourceful man who worked hard and provided for his family. He went to school for the first grade and on the very first day he climbed out the window and never went back. Everything he learned, he learned from experience. He had a head for numbers and he never forgot anything that had to do with money. If you owed him a dollar, he never forgot it. He was an honest man and he expected honesty from everyone else. He was a man of his word and taught his children to be the same, giving the phrase, "honor is priceless and glad be he who has it" extra meaning in our home.

My mother was and still is my hero. She was a woman of action and taught her children to be responsible and work with their hands. Because of her, every one of her children knew what hard work was.

It would seem luck was on my side. Apparently, there is life after death. I had parents who loved me. I lived in paradise. What else could a person ask for?

# Chapter 2
# Paradise

*"You don't develop courage by being happy in your relationships every day. You develop it by surviving difficult times and challenging adversity." Epicurus, Philosopher of the 4th century BC*

With World War 2 touching our little island, our luck began to change. Even so, my father was prepared. He had anticipated hard times and stocked the basic necessities—water, food, candles, firewood, that sort of stuff—for our family in one of the many natural caves tucked into the landscape. When the bombs began to drop, we would head for the caves and wait them out. From a child's point of view, the trip was like a field trip or an excursion. I'm sure the adults thought differently. My parents accepted life as it was and what could they do? Talk someone out of war? Hitler perhaps? Mussolini? No. They did what they had to do to protect their family and remain in good standing on the island. For the most part, it worked. We lived between our home and the caves and we had somewhat of a routine. I was only a young child and as long as my parents were there, I was content. Life continued. My father was still an influential man on the island. We still had food to eat and a roof over our heads. Some weren't so lucky. There were days when four air strikes would occur. In some ways, I'm surprised anything was left standing on the island.

Mussolini wanted everyone to speak Italian rather than Greek, so the schools started language classes. He also offered money or goods to Greeks who would claim to be Italian rather than Greek. Mussolini, called Leros "the Corregidor of the Mediterranean." He knew how important the island was for the Italian Navy in the eastern Aegean Sea. The one thing he didn't mess with, was our churches. He left those alone.

The Greek Orthodox Church used to be Catholic, but, Greeks decided to pull away from the Catholic church. We are still very similar with one major difference. Catholics call the pope his holiness. No one in this world is holy, not even the pope. Yes, he should be respected, but he is not holy. The Greek Orthodox church has bishops, but they are not his holiness. Most likely this belief is where the phrase, "even if you are a priest, you get in line," has its roots. You don't get special privileges—not even a priest. Only God gets to be called holy.

Mussolini let us keep our church. If a Greek youth was killed, he could be buried according to our church and our customs, and he did not have to buried by an Italian priest. Now, if an Orthodox priest wasn't available, then an

Italian priest could do the ceremony. Or vice versa. We were okay with that as long as a priest was there to oversee the burial.

Another difference is, Catholic priests don't get married. In the Greek Orthodox church, priests have to be married. They need the experience of being a husband and a father, so they know how to lead their congregation. The only exceptions are those who are aiming to be archbishops. Then they are to remain like Paul, single and devoted to the church.

During the war, a submarine went under the mountain then rose up inside of it. No one could find it. Radar wasn't a thing yet, so ships would hide in the natural harbors and stay safe from being attacked. That worked well until a German plane passed over Lakki. When the pilot saw the ships hiding, he called in reinforcements. The Germans sent 25 bombers and while they were bombing, they sunk the ship Vasilissa Olga, which was transporting members of the Long-Range Desert Group—a reconnaissance and raiding unit of the British Army. Today there is a monument in honor of the destroyer and all that were lost. Every year there is a celebration to remember those who gave their lives. Everyone is drinking and dancing and no one wants to go home. If you haven't already figured it out, Greeks love to celebrate. Any reason will do.

When Germany won Leros, the English started bombing our little island in force. We would hear the sirens and run for the caves in the hills. I watched planes fall from the sky, on fire. We knew people were dying.

Sometimes we would hear screaming. Not everyone made it to a shelter. Some people died as they ran for shelter. Bombs were falling, and buildings were exploding. I was young, so I didn't fully understand what was happening. Even a three-year-old knows when there is danger.

We lived peacefully with the German soldiers. Italy joined Hitler's war on June 10, 1940. From that point on, soldiers were a normal part of life. In fact, soldiers would often come to our tavern for cigarettes. Occasionally a soldier would buy the cigarettes, but more often my father was given an IOU. Not that he had much of a choice in the matter. They had guns. What could he do? Of course, most never settled their tabs. I call it Hitler's war because many of the young soldiers were doing what they had to do to survive. Yes, some of the soldiers enjoyed being mean and hurting others, but most were human beings who wanted to live and let live. The young men who burned their uniforms when the war ended showed the world what they thought of the war and of Hitler. They were caught up in another man's quest for world domination. It was either survive or die. I can't blame them for wanting to survive.

Not only were German soldiers on the island, but there were also Italian soldiers, Indian soldiers, and before all these, there were English soldiers. They fought one another for control of Leros. After the war, American soldiers were there to help us.

There are nights you go to bed, and everything is normal. Yet, when you awaken, all is different. I was almost four when that happened to me. I'd gone to bed and when I was shaken awake, everything I'd known, my entire world, changed.

Startled, I opened my eyes. My mother was standing over me. "Dimitri. Get up. We must hurry."

"But, mama…"

"Shhh…quietly, my son. Listen to your mama. Put on your shorts and shirt. We must go. Papa is waiting for us." She spoke quietly in the language I grew up with, Greek.

I wiped the sleep from my eyes and pulled my shorts and shirt on as I'd been told. My sisters and brothers were also dressing all around me. We quietly followed my mother outside where my father was gathered with a few other men, women and children. He nodded toward my mother and we were all handed as much as we could carry as we were led by the moonlight to a still marina. There was a large row boat waiting for us. I have no idea who it belonged to. My father stole it. There was no time to ask for permission. More than 30 of us sat side by side, huddled together in the night as we quietly left for safer shores. I clutched my mother's dress as I watched and waited. I was afraid. My entire life had been spent on the island. I'd rarely had a reason to leave and never in the middle of the night. Once again, I clung to her dress.

The men and the older boys rowed. The only sounds were the oars dipping into the ocean and the boat slicing through the waves. All the adults were silent. No one dared to say a word. We had no idea where we were going. Or why we were taken from our beds in the middle of the night. We did know enough to be afraid and to be like the adults—silent. As much as I wanted to know where we were going, I just waited and watched, wondering as we sped across the dark, rough sea.

Only when we ran ashore on the neighboring island of Leipsoi did I over hear my father and my godfather talking. I was supposed to be sleeping. Instead, I was listening.

"Who? Who would have done such a thing?" My father said in a low voice.

"I do not know, Pablo. It would seem the Germans knew to watch you before they came to the island." I watched my godfather shake his head in disbelief.

My father continued. "It must be a Greek then. It has to be." He sighed then repeated a phrase I'd heard back home. "The crow does not take the eye out of another crow", which means, people who are the same do not hurt one another. Family shouldn't hurt family and Greeks shouldn't hurt Greeks!

"A man in your position has enemies. Men who are jealous of who you are and what you've become. I do not doubt your suspicions. You must be careful. Watch your back and the back of your family."

My mother took hold of my shoulder. I'd been caught eavesdropping. I squeezed my eyes shut. The next thing I knew, I was again being awakened by my mother's frantic whisper. "Dimitri. We must get back on the boat. Come. Hurry."

This time, I didn't question my mother. I followed our little group from the beach back to the boat where we again were cutting through the deep and treacherous waters. Instead of landing on an island similar to Leros, my father directed those who powered our row boat and we landed on a piece of rock. A big piece of black rock. A big piece of nothing.

Our food was gone. Our water supply, very small. In fact, had my father not thought ahead and brought some distilling equipment, we would have perished on that black rock. He would collect small pans of water, build a small fire from bits of dried weeds, small sticks, and driftwood, then boil enough water so we could each have a few sips. We would have died had my father not been prepared. Even with the little water we had, we were getting terribly dehydrated.

We spent 7 days and nights on that desolate piece of uninhabited wasteland. No running water. No food. No trees for shade. No fire for warmth. Nothing soft to rest our heads upon to sleep. Yet, we had much to be thankful for. We were alive. Stories were told. Songs were sung. Mostly, we rested. We didn't have the energy for much else.

I heard more of the story as the days passed. My father had a big two-way radio he used to communicate with the mainland, the ones with the bulbs that were enormous. I do not know why he was talking with the mainland. We think he was just finding out what was happening and telling the people in Greece what was happening on Leros. Even though he had the radio hidden, and the antennae was a small wire that was not obvious to anyone not looking for it, the Germans found out he had it and sent a battalion to kill us. How did they find out you ask? Good question. My father had his suspicions. I have mine.

Perhaps someone got paid for sharing information on my father. I'll leave it at that. The one thing we're sure of is it was a Greek who did the squealing. Perhaps as my godfather suggested, it was someone who was jealous of my father.

I still don't know how my father knew the Germans were coming after us. There were only four telephones on the island at that time. Who made the call? Who risked his own neck to tell my father we were in trouble? There were many men on the island who respected my father. I believe it was someone of importance who still had some influence. It had to be. Otherwise, how would they have known?

At the start of the war, or at least when the soldiers came to Leros, if you had anything the Germans said you couldn't have, you were supposed to surrender whatever it was—the list included any firearms or explosives, ammunition, different types of machinery, and two-way radios (as well as many other items). Obviously, my father did not turn his radio over to the Germans. I do not know why. I doubt I'll ever know.

Thankfully, the Germans didn't find us on the little rock island. With more than a thousand Greek islands dotting the sea, the Germans gave up their chase. They had more important things to do, like fight a war and terrorize people. Surely a black rock in the middle of the sea was better than dying at the hands of the Germans. Every day my father would dole out a little water to sustain us. Every day we watched the horizon for ships, so we might be rescued and not die of starvation or dehydration.

On the 7<sup>th</sup> day my father spotted a ship. We found twigs and dried weeds growing between the rocks. We managed to start a little fire to send a smoke signal to the ship. We watched closely, waiting to see if we had been found. A cheer went up when we saw a few smaller boats coming toward us. We would survive!

The Turkish ship's officers from which we were spotted sent smaller boats to bring us to them. We were hungry and thirsty. They gave us a very small amount of water and pieces of an orange. It was obvious we weren't the first starving, dehydrated refugees they had found. I'm sure we weren't their last.

At the time of our rescue, Turkey was neutral. Still, they were not sure what to do with us. The ship docked in Bodrum. We were asked question after question. They gave us very little food and we were treated like criminals. The Turks considered we might be spies and once again, we feared for our lives. Of course, when you think about it, our island was under the control of the Germans. So, us being spies wasn't entirely out of the question. Thankfully, we had Turkish roots.

Prior to Italy controlling Leros in 1912, Leros was under the Turkish flag. My grandfather, originally from Ioannina, often called Yannena, was the police chief of Leros and a good friend to my godfather, Bornelis. When the questioning continued, and our fate seemed doomed, my godfather produced a picture of my grandfather in his Turkish police uniform, including the infamous Turkish bashlyk, or more commonly known—hat.

He said in Turkish, "If you kill us, you might as well be killing your own countrymen." He straightened his shoulders, more angry than afraid. We had already been through so much. We were tired, hungry, in a strange country, unsure of our future and dependent upon the help of strangers. We thought we were safe and then suddenly, we were not. It was frustrating. We had jumped from one bad situation to another.

"What? What is the meaning of this?" He threw up his hands, the picture of my grandfather gripped between his fingers.

He showed them the picture to prove we were not spies. Once they understood we had roots in Turkey, they treated us with much more respect. We were given bread, olives, and halva among other foods. After only having a few pieces of an orange, I felt as though I was feasting.

We were there three days while the Turkish officials decided what should be done with us. We boarded a train—not a passenger train but a cattle train. We were squeezed in among the cows and horses with other refugees. We huddled together as best we could while the animals moved around us. My mother was constantly cautioning us to be careful not to be stepped on and of the animal droppings. They were everywhere. Waking up with a large cow pie right next to your nose wasn't exactly a pleasant experience.

There were seven of us children, my mother and my father. Staying together in a crowded train car, when half of us were young children, was difficult. Yet, it wasn't a child who ended up lost. Somehow, we lost my father. My mother was calling out to him, "Pablo. Pablo. Where are you?"

What we did not know was my father was pulled aside by the English and drafted as a guard. They gave him a rifle and swore him in. He was on the same train, but not where we were. He did find us though. He was moving through the train calling out, "Sophia, Sophia." When he found us, he told my mother what had happened and that he was okay.

From Turkey we went to Syria. We were there for only a few short hours then we continued traveling by train. Finally, we stopped in Palestine, specifically Gaza Strip, which was our home for the duration of the war.

# Chapter 3
# Refugees

*"Since we cannot change reality, let us change the eyes which see reality." Nikos Kazantzakis, Writer of the 20th century*

I left paradise and ended up in the desert. Sometimes that happens in life. Not everyone will end up in a refugee camp, but, I guarantee, something will go wrong in life. It is not what happens to you that counts. It is how you react that defines you.

Upon arriving in Palestine, all I could see were long rows of tents. Well, tents and sand. After many days of traveling by train, with animals all around us, the tents didn't look too bad. At least we had a place to call our own, a place we could be a family again. There is a saying I have come to love, home is where my family is. We may have been in a strange place, living in a strange house, far away from the people we knew, but we had each other. That was very true in Gaza Strip. We were together. We were home.

We were taken into larger tents where all our information: name, birth city, that sort of thing, was written down and filed away. The English were in charge and they were very good at keeping things organized. We were given identification cards which we were supposed to carry with us all the time. I'm sure my parents had mine.

Once the people in charge had our information, they led us to another area where my parents were interviewed, basically, to see what they could do, how they could be of help in the camp. It takes many people to keep a city of refugees running smoothly. My father had already been assigned as a guard on the train, so he continued in that role in the refugee camp. We were glad because his job meant he was nearly always close by, usually guarding the gate. Refugees were allowed to leave the camp if they had money and were going shopping at the local stores. Not everyone had money though and not everyone left or entered the camp having good motives. We were there for our safety, not as prisoners. Although, I'm sure there were some who felt as if they were prisoners. If a person chooses to look at life with bitterness, then a mansion would seem like a prison. Others can see a refugee camp as heaven. Remember to look for the good things in life.

After leaving the identification tent, we were then taken to a makeshift hospital tent where we were cleaned up and checked for diseases. Once we all passed a rudimentary check-up, we were taken to our new home, a tent no bigger than an average family room was our home for the next 3 years.

My mother was pregnant and taking care of 7 children. She gave birth to a little boy. He was sick and without proper medical facilities, he died. The doctors did what they could with what they had. There was a war going on. A refugee camp was low on the list for medical equipment.

We had no running water or indoor bathrooms. We had centralized facilities, both kitchen and bathroom, that everyone used. For meals, we were given some basic tools, some bowls, plates, spoons etc. We didn't necessarily need cooking supplies because we didn't prepare our own meals. We were, however, given a pot which we would take to the centralized kitchen to fill from the much larger pot which fed everyone in the camp. We didn't ask, "what is on the menu?" We didn't complain.

We ate what we were given. For three years, every single day, we ate some sort of soup. Occasionally there was meat in the pot. There were always potatoes, lots of potatoes, in the mix. We didn't ask what it was or groan when it looked like what we'd just eaten the day before, and the day before that. We just ate it and hoped for the best. Sometimes people would get sick from the food. With so many people to feed and the government shipping food, you can understand how some food might go bad. Storing large quantities of food was difficult and because of that, we received foods that would be easier to store like big bags of potatoes.

The bathrooms were made of wood and offered some privacy but not much in the way of safety. They were similar to what is known as outhouses in that they were positioned over a hole. One day a baby was crawling around and managed to fall in the bathroom hole. The baby died.

A little down from the centralized bathrooms was the garbage dump. Even refugees have garbage and to keep some order of cleanliness to the camp, everyone was required to dispose of their garbage in the large hole provided.

There were fences all around the camp, keeping us separate from the Palestinians and Arabs. My father guarded the gate and often we would play near there. On the other side of the gate lived a wealthy old man. I believe he was somewhere around 110 years old. He was wealthy because he owned land, horses and camels, and he was a farmer. He grew carrots, tomatoes, watermelons and other produce. I especially remember the watermelon. They were so big he would carry two on a camel, one on each side, to transport them. They were triple the size of the watermelons we see today. He would take his sword and just touch the watermelon and it would split open. After eating soup day after day, the watermelon was like eating dessert. He fell in love with us and by the time the war was over, we called him Grandpa.

We had no toys in the refugee camp—no balls or cars to play with. So, we had to come up with our own games. We took pieces of rags and filled them with dirt, or whatever we could find, then tied up the corners to make a sort of ball. Then we'd kick it to each other or throw it back and forth like a baseball. It was crude, but it was something to play with. Then, we would take sticks and use rubber bands and wire and make our own sling shots.

We were careful to not shoot the ladies. But we had plenty of targets to shoot at. I'm pretty sure I never got into trouble with my sling shot. Kids are resilient. I was no different. We made the best of whatever situation we were in and we still managed to have fun.

Wind storms were new to us. I had never experienced a storm that caused sand to blow everywhere. They were powerful storms. If you opened your mouth, you'd have a mouth full of sand. Open your eyes and your mama would be washing them out, trying to get the sand out. I couldn't see anything when one of those storms happened. It was best to stay in your tent until the storm passed.

My mom's uncle was also a refugee and a storm lifted his whole tent. He tried to hang onto the tent, but the wind was so strong, it lifted him up too. He fell, and he died from the fall. The tents weren't secured very well to the ground. The stakes could come out and if they did, then everything would be a mess and many things would be missing because the wind would carry them off.

In the beginning of this chapter, I mentioned I'd left paradise and ended up in the desert. Sometimes, paradise stops being paradise, even if for just a short while. By being in the refugee camp, where we had food to eat and shelter to protect ourselves from the weather, we were spared from what was happening in Greece during the war.

Once Germany conquered a country, they did not consider themselves to be responsible for the people's well-being. Food, not their concern. Water, not their problem. The Germans killed their cattle and stole their milk. They confiscated their boats, so they couldn't even fish. People were starving all over Greece. The people would stand in line for a chance to dig in the garbage dumps for food. Others would dig through the trash of the Germans or Italians. People would dump their dead relatives in the gutters, so they wouldn't have to give up their bread card. Doing so would have meant less food in a household that was already starving. Bodies were lying in the streets. 6 million Greeks died of starvation during World War II. The Germans stole everything the International Red Cross brought in.

The only reason Leros was spared this agony, was because the Italians controlled the island during the war. While conditions in Leros weren't what they used to be, they were still much better than what our countrymen were facing on the mainland. A refugee camp was paradise compared to what our fellow Greeks endured.

# Chapter 4
# Homecoming

*"Good people do not need laws to tell them to act responsibly, while bad people will find a way around the laws." Plato, Philosopher of the 5th century BC*

1946 brought the end of the war and we set off on our journey home. We traveled in much the same way we arrived. I was older, more aware of what was going on around me.

We traveled by ship to the island of Kalymnos and then went by barge to our home, or what was left of our home, on Leros. As we approached the island there were two ships nearby. On one, a flag was blowing in the breeze. There was something about that flag, something that attracted me to it. I knew that flag brought freedom and whatever that flag represented, I wanted. I can't tell you how I knew. There was just something about it. Something proud. Something bold. I knew there was something special about that flag. I didn't know until later the red, white, and blue flag with stars and stripes represented The United States of America.

Later, when the soldiers were helping us on the island, giving us toothpaste, vitamins, brushes, and things like this, I saw a picture of the promised land. People were making tires and they were smiling. They had these metal tubes with water shooting out of them. It looked like heaven to me. No one had to carry five-gallon buckets to get water? Water came straight out of a pipe? Was everyone in America rich? Did a person snap their fingers and the water flowed?

The flag pierced my heart. The pictures made the longing nearly unbearable.

The entire island of Leros had been affected in some way by the bombs. Buildings were in rubble. Houses gone. People dead. Everyone had been touched in some way by the war. Including us.

One picture that has remained with me all these years is former German soldiers lighting their uniforms on fire. They didn't want to be associated with Hitler, or with the gestapo. They didn't want to go to war. They hated what they did, what they were ordered to do. For many of them, it was either go to war or be shot themselves. They had no choice. So many young men who were fighting for Hitler started cleaning the streets of Leros. They opened warehouses to give people supplies and tried to help the people who lived there however they could. A lot of the soldiers felt terrible for being part of such evil. They were human beings who were caught in a horrible place—not war mongers.

When I was younger, when the soldiers first came to Leros, I was afraid of them. I had heard talk, if a person didn't do what they say, they would just kill them. After the war, I saw them for who they were. People. People who lived and breathed, loved and laughed, just like me.

Many people were made rich because of the war. War always brings about more business. The DuPont Family earned their millions by supplying gun powder during the Civil War. By World War I, the DuPont's were the only suppliers of gun powder to the United States. The Delano Family, as in Franklin Delano Roosevelt, made their fortune in providing Opium to the Union Army to treat soldiers. Every war has seen rags to riches success stories. Unfortunately, this story will not be one of them. Then again, I don't think I'd change my past. I don't know how that would change my future and I love my life.

Thankfully, we all survived the refugee camp. We didn't die on a black rock, we weren't claimed by the sea, and we didn't become a statistic in a refugee camp. We were back in paradise. We arrived home ready to get on with our lives, to pick up where we left off, but, we no longer had a home to return to. And no, our home wasn't flattened by a bomb. When we approached our home, we realized something wasn't quite right. Someone was living there.

In Leros, back in those days, any kind of deal—even a land deal—was based on a handshake and the word of the person making the deal. There were no titles. No deeds. Just a person's honor. Now, the other side of the island, the side the Italians were rebuilding, those properties came with paperwork. We weren't so lucky.

My father found himself curious but didn't get angry. Instead, he knocked on the front door. A woman answered. Her husband had made a deal with my father, but he was no longer around to back up my father's claim he bought the house. Her husband had died sometime between us fleeing Leros and coming back. She wanted to see proof of the sale. My father had none. The woman's husband was my father's best man at his wedding. Her husband was the godfather to one of my brothers or sisters. In other words, he and my father were in good relationship, they knew a handshake was all they'd ever need to make a deal between them. But, we had no proof. She needed a place to live too. And back then, and still sometimes today, ladies had no idea about the business of their husbands. She just didn't know. We had no home. There was nothing we could do. In Lakki, the Italians made sure everyone had a deed to their property. We weren't so lucky.

From May through September there is no rain on Leros and the temperatures are very warm. It was a good thing too because for three weeks we slept on the ground outside the house we used to own. We had nowhere else to go. What were we supposed to do? No one helped us. We even had family on the island. Yet, no one helped. I don't know why. Perhaps they were jealous of my father because he was wealthy before the war. I tend to believe that is why we had to leave Leros in the first place, someone was jealous of my father.

# Jimmy the Greek

My aunt and uncle, they had plenty of room in their house, but they didn't let us stay there. They had one room that was painted with oil paint. They kept the room like a showroom, you could look but not touch. We could have easily slept on the floor in that room, but the room was too good for us. My aunt didn't want us in that room, so we slept on the ground.

We had no home, we were living outside. We didn't have much of anything including clothes and even if we did, we didn't have the proper tools to clean them. I started getting bullied at school. Not a lot, but a little bit. One kid used to bug me all the time, and I remember him because his mouth stunk—he had bad teeth. Every day he picked a fight with me. I tried to get him to leave me alone, but he wouldn't. This guy still lives in Leros. He's a produce man now. We nod and say hi when I go back to visit. We have no problems now. I don't hold grudges. I still remember, but I don't hold grudges.

My father began looking for a house for us to live in. We couldn't sleep in this woman's yard forever. There was a café owner, he had a little business making coffees, that sort of thing. He was so cheap it was pathetic. But, he had a house that was empty. He came and gave my father the keys and told him we could stay for as long as we needed to, for free. He might have been cheap, but he had a good heart. Our own people didn't help us, but this stranger did. He said to my father, "Pablo, take your kids, take your family, and go live in my house." He didn't have to do that. Family is supposed to look after family. Sometimes that doesn't happen.

When we returned from Leros my father had no job. We had no source of income and he had 9 mouths to feed. The tavern was no longer ours. The gambling house, somewhere else. The cigarette factory, no longer running. The wine vats, someone else's. Everything was gone. My father started working making musical instruments. He made instruments similar to lutes, and cimbaloms. He made santouris, which are large stringed instruments—between 120 and 140 strings—which are played with a cotton covered hammer, like a hammer dulcimer. Not many people can play these instruments today.

He not only made the instruments, he played them as well, which is how he had met my mother long before the war. He traveled to the island of Nisyros to play for a wedding. He met my mother, they got married and they came to Leros to start a family. My mother had eight children, one who died in the refugee camp, but she also had miscarriages. If all her children had lived she would have had twelve children. I got my love of music from my dad and my older brother. Music has a way of bringing joy into a person's life, even when times are hard.

After the war, my father hired a lawyer and ended up getting a settlement from the loss of payment from the German army for all the IOU's they owed. He didn't get much, but it was something.

Since I try to always see the positive in every situation, there were several good things about not having our own house back.

Do you remember the stories about your grandparents walking a mile through the snow uphill both ways just to get to school? Well, believe it or not, before the war we had to do that too. Maybe not to get to school and maybe not through snow, okay, definitely not through snow, but we did have to walk for miles on rough terrain up and down a mountain just to get water. Every single day we would have to carry buckets and get enough water for cooking, cleaning, washing clothes, bathing, and for drinking. My feet were like leather. When we moved, we still had to bring water to our house, but we were much closer—in fact, we were right next to the water supply. Kids make the best of everything and I was no different.

At least we didn't have to clean bathrooms. Well, we didn't have an inside bathroom. We would dig a hole and put some wood or whatever else we could find to build a little privacy wall. We'd go to the bathroom in the hole and when we were done we'd cover our waste with dirt.

We would do whatever chores our mother would tell us to. I would catch chickens or rabbits, run to the store or a neighbor's house, run errands—anything that had to be done. Afterward, rain or shine, we'd play in the mountains and by the shore. We'd pretend we were at war and ambush each other from behind the rocks and from the inside of caves. We made up lots of games to keep us busy.

We learned to make our own movies. We set up a white sheet and we used candles to cast shadows on the sheet. We used a stick to make a human being and we created stories. We would set up rocks, so the viewers could sit down. Of course, we charged a fee. What movie house didn't charge?

As you can imagine, playing outside we got really dirty. My mom had a giant tub, a pot really. And once a week we would fill the pot and all the children would take baths. Living close to the water source made this job a whole lot easier. I always wanted to bathe first. You can imagine why.

Another bonus of living in a new home was we were so much closer to the sea. You could look out a window and see the water. Which made the water a much more tempting way to pass the time. We had no televisions or radios—no electronics to entertain us. We had to entertain ourselves.

One day some friends and I wanted to go swimming. Now, we didn't own swimming trunks, so we swam naked. There weren't any tourists back then and not many people had time to go swimming, so it wasn't a big deal. No one saw us and if they did, they didn't say anything. We were just kids being kids. Well, we would swim and cool off then we'd lie down in the sand in the warm sun to dry off and rest.

Another kid, around our age, wanted to join us so he dropped his pants, thought he had to fart but he must have had a bellyache or something so he just well, instead of farting, he pooped, right there. Right in front of us. He took off running with his pants and we all ran for the ocean. It's a good thing he was gone when we got out of the water because we would have kicked his butt.

Today on the beaches on Leros you'd be arrested for indecent exposure. The tourists have found our beaches and spend as much time there as they can. Leros is happy. Tourists mean more income for the people.

One summer my brother, Tony, and I were swimming by the pier across the street from our house. Again, it was before tourists were regular visitors on Leros. He swam under water and scratched me where he shouldn't have been scratching so I put my hand down and held his head under water.

My mother had been on the steps of the house, she must have been shaking rugs or something, and she had been watching us at the same time. When I let him go, he came up out of the water choking and coughing and making a scene—like he was dying or something.

I looked up and saw my mother heading our way. By the look on her face I knew I wouldn't get a chance to explain so I just started running. Buck naked, I ran. And I ran some more. She ran right behind me. I ran for a good mile and a half, through the streets of Leros. Naked as could be. I would have kept running too but I passed a guy and he reached out and grabbed me and held me until my mother caught up to us. She whipped my butt the entire way home. Holding my arm with one hand and hitting my butt with the other, all the way back through the streets of Leros until we got back to the beach. My rear end was the color of a watermelon.

We finally got back to the beach where Tony made the mistake of saying, "Mama, I was faking it. I wasn't choking." She let go of me and grabbed him and started beating him. Me and Tony, we were close. I don't think I could sit down for a week!

Corporal punishment was normal in Leros. As kids, we'd get spanked by both our parents and our teachers. Probably our next-door neighbors too if we needed it.

I remember my teacher hitting me one time. I don't remember exactly what I did, although I believe it had to do with me not memorizing my lessons. We always had to memorize our lessons and if we didn't, well, we'd get hit by the teacher. I went home, and I told my mother about what happened. Perhaps I was expecting sympathy. She looked at me then turned around and went outside. She came back with a long piece of wood, a stick from a tree, and she started beating me. After she finished she said, "When you go to school, your teacher is your mother and your father. You do what she says." That's it. I got no sympathy at all. I got in more trouble at home than I did from the teacher. That was the last time I got whipped at school.

When I visited Leros I saw some of my former teachers walking around. I hugged and kissed them, then thanked them for all they did. I told them, "You beat the living crap out of me and helped make me what I am today. Thank you!" Sometimes you don't see how good something can be until much later—after the situation has passed and the pain is nothing but a memory.

Having a toothache in Leros could be a painful experience—not just from the tooth. I was about 10 and my tooth was killing me. My father told me to go to a friend of his, a dentist. I went, and I told him where my mouth was hurting. He didn't put me in the chair. He didn't check it out or look in my mouth. He just put me in a headlock, the guy with him put some sort of thing in my mouth to keep it open, then he used a pair of pliers and ripped two teeth out of my mouth. Then he told me to go home.

I ran home, crying and bleeding. I remember the room. He had the chair and instruments. He had a drill and the foot pedal. He had everything there...but he didn't use them. And he called himself a dentist?

I went to school with Stella. In fact, I lived near her. Her father was the barber. We didn't have a lot of money to pay for haircuts, but we couldn't go to school looking scraggly, it wasn't allowed. Even if it had been, my mother would never have allowed it. Before school one year, I went for my haircut. Stella's dad would cut the boys hair all the way down to the scalp. That year, instead of giving me the normal haircut, he played a joke on me and made a crisscross cut on the top of my head. The rest of my hair was sticking out like a porcupine. We had a good laugh over that haircut.

We managed to pay our pennies for our haircuts. My mother knew education would change our lives. My brother, Steve, and I loved school, we loved to learn. She didn't have to tell us more than once it was time to get up. The rest of my brothers and sisters needed a little more convincing.

You would think living on an island, I would know how to swim. But, I didn't. I managed to get cooled off and mess around with friends in the water without learning to swim. When I joined the boy scouts, the members of our troop learned that me and a few other guys couldn't swim. So, one day on an excursion we took an air boat to another island close by. It wasn't more than a piece of rock. We were rowing and rowing and I was getting tired. We were almost there and, well, I wasn't expecting it, but the troop leader picked me up and threw me in the water. I made it to the island. Well, I collapsed on the shore of the island, but I knew how to swim.

It seemed we were always hungry when I was little. Food was scarce. We raised chickens and rabbits in our back yard to help feed our family. They would run around the yard enjoying their freedom. Those were smart chickens. I'm pretty sure I haven't seen any as smart since. They'd be calm, just enjoying the day until my mother would say, "Jimmy, we're gonna have soup." As soon as those words came out of her mouth, those chickens would scatter. Feathers were flying. Chickens were squawkin'. They knew one of them was going to end up in the soup pot.

I'd have to chase one of them down, cut her neck and clean it so we could eat. The rabbits had no idea what was going to happen, but those chickens, they were smart. Maybe those rabbits weren't so dumb after all. Perhaps they had a plan because I'll still eat chicken, I'm used to it. But I won't eat rabbit.

I guess I've always had a way with animals. When we lived in the free rental house, there was a little convenience store close to us. The owner, a lady, was always busy doing something for her store. She made yogurt and took care of customers. Well, she had a donkey. He would hide out behind two walls that separated the store and the church and the road. He was very friendly, and I liked him a lot.

Every time I passed by, she would hand me a bucket and she'd yell, "Marino (that was the Donkey's name). Dimitris is here. Go to the fountain and he'll give you a drink." When the donkey heard her scream, he would run to the fountain all by himself. He knew exactly where to go. I would be waiting for him with a drink. When he drank all he wanted, he'd run back behind the wall. He was trained, and he trusted me. Just like the chickens, except the trust part. He was listening. But, he had no fear of being turned into soup.

Christmas on Leros was a celebration. We were very religious people and church was important to us. Stella's father was very talented, and he would make homemade ornaments for the tree. He even made a wooden nativity set and a copy of the church above their house on the hill. It was very beautiful.

My brother used to bring home a little Christmas tree and we would put little ornaments on the tree made from Christmas cards. He put a light on the bottom and it would shine up in the tree and make it light up. We didn't get presents. We didn't have any money for gifts. Sometimes we would get a penny which made us very happy. We could buy some candy or fruit, or maybe a small toy. A penny at Christmas was something to be grateful for.

We learned how to make a little bit of money at Christmas time. We would go around and sing Christmas carols. If we were the first ones to sing at a door, then sometimes whoever lived there would open the door, invite us in and maybe give us a penny. We made a lot of money singing. Of course, a lot of money back then is not much these days.

We lived next door to a cemetery—an English cemetery—in Leros. When the soldiers would die, they would need a place to bury their dead, so we have German Cemeteries, English Cemeteries, Italian, and Greek cemeteries. After the war the Germans exhumed the bodies of their dead and took them back to Germany, but the English are still buried where they died. They send someone from the government to take care of the stones and the grounds. We would run and play in the cemetery. The headstones were in English, so I couldn't read the names, but we'd still pretend to know who was in each grave.

My friends would say, "Doesn't it creep you out? Living next to a cemetery?" I told them, "No, I don't fear the dead. I'm more worried about the living."

# Chapter 5
# The Dream

*"Small opportunities are often the beginning of great enterprises." Demosthenes, Orator of the 4th century BC*

Shortly after we returned to Leros from Palestine, my father's brother contacted him. He and his wife were living in New York City, NY, and could not have any children. They wanted to adopt a child. After talking it over, my parents agreed to let them adopt my sister, Irene. He and my uncle prepared all the paperwork, got everything ready and the adoption was approved. The only problem was, someone had to escort my sister across the Atlantic to the United States.

In 1947 my father left with my sister for New York City, NY. It took them 17 nights and days to cross the ocean on a converted war ship. My father, being a musician, was the entertainer on the crossing. They would drink some beer and my father would play the lute. The captain would chat with him a little in English. When my father was in Palestine, he learned a few English words and phrases, so he knew more English than any of the other passengers. He became the official translator, not that he was fluent in English.

Well, one man loved to hear my father play the lute, so he was with him all the time. Every time my father would play, he would be there right beside him. One evening, after my father played, this man said, "Pablo, I need a favor. I see you have good relationship with the captain. You're a good interpreter. Would you ask the doctor to give me something to help me go to the bathroom? I'm constipated." He hadn't been able to go to the bathroom for days.

My father, being a good friend, wanted to help so he took the man to the doctor and my father tried to explain the situation. His words weren't enough, so he was pointing to his butt and using his hands to show the expression, nothing, nothing came out in seven days.

The doctor was laughing so hard, but he got the point. He gave my father a box of stool softeners and told him the instructions. The only problem was, my father didn't understand the instructions, so he just told the guy to take the medicine.

The guy took the medicine alright, he took all the medicine—at one time. A little while later, his stomach started gurgling and convulsing. He ran for the bathroom. For the next 6 days all he did was run to the bathroom. The captain gave him his own bathroom to use and he came to be called "The Shit Man." A woman told the whole story in a book she was writing. I have no idea if the book was ever published.

Afterward the guy came up to my father and said, "You are a very good interpreter."

Once settled in the United States, my father began working as a builder designing restaurant bars. He made $10 a week. He petitioned for us to come to the United States to join him. Things were different then. We went to Athens to visit the American Embassy, so they could check us out, make sure we were inoculated, healthy, that sort of thing. While we waited to be approved, life went on in Leros.

My father sent money back to the island, so we could buy groceries and have money for everyday living. My mother took care of the children and our home. Back then women were discouraged from visiting the town square. If a woman lived on one side of the square and she needed to get to the other side, she would have to walk all the way around the square. If a husband saw his wife walking through the square it would be an embarrassment to him and he would sometimes beat her when he went home. Not all husbands did this, but some.

Since the postman delivered mail to the square, my mother was unable to get the mail herself. So, my uncle would get our mail for us, including my father's checks. He was supposed to cash them, take money to pay our running tab at the grocery store he owned, then give my mother the rest, but he never did. He cashed the check and yet somehow our bill at his grocery store never went down.

One time she sent me to the store for some sugar. She wanted to bake something. When I got to the store he told me, "tell your mother you cannot get sugar. The bill is too high." Then he had one of his workers throw me out of the store. I went back and told my mother. There was nothing my mother could do. She was trying to survive in Leros. My father was in the United States.

A man who had been in the grocery store overheard what happened, so he went to the other grocery store and told the owner. That man sent us some sugar, but my mother refused to accept the gift. She said, "Take it back. We don't need the sugar." She was too proud. We didn't need charity. We would survive without sweets.

This uncle was married to my father's sister. He wasn't a kind man. He and his wife knew we had nothing to eat. We maybe had one small meal a day, if that. We were hungry. For some reason I was sent to his home. Perhaps to get a letter or something from my father. My uncle was eating a large plate of macaroni. To this day I remember how hungry I was and how much I wanted some of the food on his plate. I was a child. Yet, he didn't feed me. He didn't pay any attention to me. They ate, and no one talked to me. Now, when my wife makes macaroni, I'm the first one at the table and I'm gobbling it up!

One of my mother's sisters got together with my aunt, the one who wouldn't give me any food, and wrote letters to my father in New York City. They told him my mother was a putana, the Italian word for whore. Why would they do that? Were they still jealous of my mother and father? Did they want to hurt her? Or my father? My mother was taking care of seven children—by herself, in a small house. When could she have men come in to our home? Even if she had been, and I don't think she was, they shouldn't have done something like that. I don't know why they would.

I don't hold grudges. But, I don't forget either.

School in Greece, while my father was in the United States, was rough. Because my father lived in the US and supposedly sent us money, everyone thought we were rich. We didn't walk around blabbing about not receiving our money, we just endured. While in school, we were supposed to receive something to eat. Usually, it was raisin bread and a little cacao, or what is known as hot chocolate in the United States. The teachers refused to give us some. There was a priest, a very smart, fair priest who noticed everyone eating but us. He pulled the leader aside and told him, "Just because their father is in the United States doesn't mean they're rich. You need to give them something to eat." So, they started giving us some.

After four and a half years we were approved to go to the United States. I was 13 years old and I was finally following the red, white and blue flag to the land where dreams come true.

We first travelled to Athens to get our paperwork and our examinations and shots. They were very strict. America didn't want immigrants to bring diseases and sickness to their country. If someone was sick, they weren't allowed to enter the United States and would be sent back to the original country at the ship's expense. The owners of the ships didn't want that to happen, so they had doctors examine each person to make sure they were in good health. Thankfully, we were all healthy.

We travelled on a repurposed war ship in bunks and hammocks that two could sleep in, in the belly of the ship. There wasn't any entertainment. No luxury accommodations. No first-class cabins with comfortable beds. But, we were on our way to America. That was enough.

We were at sea 17 days and nights. My sister, Maria, and I were the only two in our family who didn't get sea sick. So, we explored the ship together. There wasn't much else to do. We would walk around for hours. Many days there would be rain, so we wandered around inside the ship.

The ship had a diesel engine—it was very loud. I wanted to learn more, so a guide took me to visit the engine room. I wondered how the engine worked and what was making all the noise. The shafts were naked, so a person could see all the action. One piston would come down while another one went up. It was fascinating to watch the engineers work.

Besides Greeks, there were Italians and maybe a few other nationalities traveling with us. Most of the passengers were Greek and Italian. One Italian man decided he'd had enough boredom, so he offered a prize—his valuable watch—to the winner of a talent show.

Everyone got excited. There were musicians, singers, magicians, dancers, you name it, and people were practicing. The prize would be nice but having something to do would probably have been incentive enough. We were all looking forward to the entertainment.

There was a famous Greek entertainer traveling with us to America. His name was Nikos Gounaris. He began playing the mandolin when he was four years old and he attended the Conservatory of Music in Athens. He was a composer and went on to write more than 400 songs in his career as a professional musician. He was one of the most famous entertainers in all of Greece and he was traveling with us on the ship.

The night of the talent show arrived, and people were producing costumes and props, borrowing from each other as needed, to put on the best show they could produce with what they had.

Toward the end of the program some Greek music began to play. We were all watching to see who was coming on next when four women dressed in belly dancing clothes arrived carrying a litter holding Nikos Gounaris dressed in clothes fit for an Arabian King. Another woman dressed in dance clothes was playing a drum as they walked from behind the curtain. We all started clapping and laughing. We didn't care who won the watch. We were being entertained by a world class musician. He sang, and the women danced to entertain us. Yes, he won the watch, but he deserved it. It was a wonderful night that I've not forgotten. The rest of the trip wasn't so bad after that. We had a lot of fun just remembering the different performances.

When I learned Nikos died from cancer in 1965, I was saddened. But, I am very thankful I had the opportunity to see him perform live—even if it was on a repurposed war ship full of immigrants heading to America.

The rest of the time on the ship we spent exploring or playing a homemade version of jacks. We'd throw up a stone and pick more stones up before the stone we threw up dropped. We did what we could to keep our minds and hands occupied. Sometimes we played shuffleboard. We did watch the movie Pinocchio. We enjoyed seeing it. It really was a grand adventure.

As we got closer to America, we started seeing more birds, mostly seagulls. I decided I wanted to catch a bird, so I found a piece of string and a nail and tied the string to the nail, like fishline and a hook. I bent the nail and attached a small piece of bread to it, like a hook with bait. As soon as I started casting my piece of string, the birds starting diving for the bread. Most of them got the bread off the nail with no problem, but one got hooked on the nail and I reeled him in—just like a fish. My mother—and everyone else—saw the whole thing. The others were complaining saying I shouldn't have done something like that. My mother came to me and I unhooked the bird and sent him on his way. I have no idea whether he lived or died. My attention, and everyone else's, turned to a growing landscape on the horizon.

# Chapter 6
# America, newly arrived

*"I know that each one of us travels to love*
*alone, alone to faith and to death. I know it.*
*I've tried it. It doesn't help. Let me come with*
*you." Giannis Ritsos, Poet of the 20th century*

"I see it! I see land!" We were all standing on deck watching for shore. Word had circulated that day would be the day we'd see land. We'd see America. For most of us, it was a dream come true. We had no idea what to expect and perhaps our expectations were not quite realistic. It did not matter. I was 13. But inside, I was remembering the red, white, and blue flag and everything it represented for me.

Suddenly everyone stopped complaining. We could see the statue of liberty in the distance. Everyone forgot what I'd done. They stopped thinking about the poor bird. We were almost to America. We made it!

The captain began explaining to us what we could expect when we pulled into port. We were some of the very few immigrants to come through a port in Newark, New Jersey. Most immigrants passed through Ellis Island in New York City or Philadelphia.

We had to go through the same type of inspections as Ellis Island and Philadelphia though. We were first given a medical examination. Thankfully, none of us had developed any illness during the crossing which kept us from entering America. Then we had an eye examination. If an immigrant was allowed to come to America, then it was expected they would go to work to support themselves and not become a burden on society. Until they found a job, their sponsor was responsible for their care. There was no welfare system. Back then, it was thought if a person was going blind, they could not support themselves. We also had to undergo mental and legal examinations to make sure we were entering the country sane and that we were legal immigrants and not stole-a-ways. We were also investigated to make sure we were not wanted for crimes in our own countries. The last part of the process—showing we had $20 in our pockets to start our life in the United States with. A law passed in 1909 requiring each immigrant to have at least $20. Once we passed through all the hoops we had to jump through, we could collect our luggage and enter the United States. We had a whole pile of luggage. They let you bring a lot of stuff onto the ship.

When I stepped onto American soil, I knelt down and kissed the ground. This, this is what I had dreamed of. I was 13 and I didn't care what anyone thought. I had dreamt of this day and I was thankful.

# Jimmy the Greek

My father and uncle came for us in a pick-up truck and took us to Hoboken, New Jersey. I was completely in awe of everything around me. The cars I'd seen in Greece were tiny. The ones in America were huge. The buildings were so tall, and people were everywhere, doing all sorts of things. Walking, talking, laughing—their excitement was contagious.

The apartment we lived in was furnished very nice, like my dining room now. Table cloth, flowers, candles, all very nice. Our apartment was in a Greek neighborhood around 101$^{st}$ Street and Lexington Avenue, which is the beginning of Harlem.

We arrived in the fall. My father had been living with a beautiful lady. Her husband was old and well, they needed one another. I'm not saying it's right, but it is what it is. He bought an apartment for a $1000.00. Today, that same apartment would be a whole lot more.

When we went to the apartment ladies from the church were there waiting on us hand and foot—like they were our servants or something. I thought, what the hell is going on? Is this how we're going to live in America? Will people be waiting on us all the time? What has my father done? Has he become rich?

We sat down and the ladies brought us soup, then a delicious meal, and soda. It was the first time I ever drank Coca-Cola. That was back when there was cocaine in the soda. It was tasty. It's funny how you remember certain small details from the past.

The next morning, when I woke up, the same ladies were there again. Serving us pancakes, eggs, orange juice, and all I could think was, "Wow! This is the life! This beats anything we had on Leros!"

The next day I woke up and I didn't smell bacon cooking. I couldn't hear voices. There was no food made. No waitresses. No cooks in the kitchen. Nobody but us. I asked my mom, "What happened?"

My dad said, "From now on you'll be doing all the work. So, we made our own breakfast with whatever food we had. We cleaned. We did the dishes. We washed our own clothes in the bathtub by using a plunger then we squeezed the water out of the clothes by hand. In a lot of ways, life was still just as hard as when we lived on Leros. In some ways, harder. The difference was knowing we could change our circumstances in the United States. We didn't have that option in Leros.

Our clothing took a beating in Leros. We'd slide down the side of the mountain and wear holes in our pants. We'd tear our shirts on prickles. Only our shoes survived and that is because we never wore shoes! My mother had been scrimping and saving so we would have something decent to wear when we arrived in America. We may have been poor, but she had her pride. We didn't have much more than one decent outfit each, and nothing warm to wear, but our clothes were presentable. Fall and winter in New York can be downright cold.

The woman that my father had been living with helped us a lot. She met my mother then stopped her relationship with my father. My mother got sick and she helped us for almost a year while my mother was in the hospital. She had some money and her husband was sick and he died, so she helped us. She didn't have to do that. She had that much respect for my mother. Maybe she felt like she owed my mother something. I don't know. But, she was a very nice lady.

Sophia, my mother, was born on the island of Nisyros. Life was even harder for her than it was for us on Leros, or in our early days in America. When her mother died, her father took it so hard he picked up two rocks and beat himself with them until he died too. That is how much he loved my grandmother.

I don't know how my father living with another woman affected my mother. Knowing how much her parents loved each other, she must have been disappointed and hurt. But, she never said a word. She couldn't do anything about it. It was over. So, why complain? She did what she had to do. She took care of us kids and she took care of my father. She worked in the garment district and still cooked and cleaned and made sure her children were going to school and well behaved. My mother...she was an amazing woman.

# Chapter 7
# America, NYC

*"You'll come to learn a great deal if you study the Insignificant in depth." Odysseus Elytis, Poet of the 20th century*

In 1950, New York City was full of immigrants from all over the world. Vincent Richard Impellitteri, an Italian immigrant, was the newly elected mayor. On average, a house cost $8500, a car $1500, a gallon of gas was 18 cents and a loaf of bread was 17 cents.

Perry Como and Dean Martin were causing the girls to swoon by singing ballads on the radio. James Stewart, Fred Astaire, Bette Davis, and Doris Day were dancing and singing across the movie screen. The Ed Sullivan Show, You Bet Your Life, and The Howdy Doody Show entertained us on television.

There were dance halls and picture shows, bars and theaters. Shoe shines and musicians lined the sidewalks, hoping to make a few cents. Beggars and millionaires walked the same path. Street vendors dished out lunch. A million sights and sounds all combined to create the one and only New York City. No other place on earth like it. The perfect place to be a newly arrived American, which is exactly what I considered myself!

The war was over, everyone was excited. There was money to be made. Friends to meet up with. Goals to reach. The city was noisy and full of life, and I loved it. Ten years before, I was stranded on a rock, hoping to make it out. Now, here I was, the luckiest guy to be alive living in the greatest city on earth!

Living in New York City was a complete change for us. We didn't have tall buildings on Leros, we had mountains. We had no problem communicating on Leros, we lived among other Greeks who spoke the same language as we did. In NYC, we feared never being understood. There were so many different languages being spoken we figured we'd never be able to communicate. So many changes, so much to learn. Yet, everything was so exciting.

As long as I stayed in our neighborhood, I was okay. Everyone spoke Greek. But, staying in one area in New York City is like asking a Greek not to be in everybody else's business, it just wasn't going to happen. We're Greek. We talk a lot, we're loud and we have an opinion on just about everything. Haven't you seen the movie My Big Fat Greek Wedding? Of course, I wandered the city. It was calling me.

My father moved to New York City four years before I did so, he had more time to learn English. The first day we came he was talking to the landlord. I heard him, but I couldn't understand a word of what he was saying. It all sounded like babbling to me. I was in awe. My father knew how to not only speak but carry on a conversation in English. I would listen to him and besides yes and no, I couldn't understand a word. I was in awe and proud he learned English so well.

A couple of months later I learned our landlord was Italian. He spoke very little English. My father and he had been talking in a mixture of languages: Italian, Spanish, Spanish with a Puerto Rican dialect, and a bit of Greek. My father didn't know English any better than he did when we were in the refugee camp in Gaza Strip. We were doomed.

My brothers and I went exploring one evening. Some Puerto Ricans came up to us with a knife and said, give us your money. We didn't know what they were saying then, we couldn't understand them at the time, although by their actions we knew what they wanted. There are ways to express yourself without saying a word. I said, "No English." They couldn't believe we didn't speak English. I repeated it several times and finally, they knew we didn't understand so they left us alone. That was the beginning of the gangs in Harlem, from 101$^{st}$ Street to 125$^{th}$ Street in Manhattan.

There were only white Greeks living on Leros. We had one black man and his daughter living on the island. Other than them, I had never seen a black person. Or a Mexican. Or Puerto Rican. Add the different nationalities to the different languages spoken all around me in New York City, and you can imagine how confused I was. It took me a while to learn what was what and who was who. New York City may be the most diversified place on earth and I was plunked down in the middle of it all.

We had to learn how things were done in New York City, and that included things we did all our lives, like eat lunch at school. My father didn't make much money. He was still making $10 per week and we were nearly always hungry.

Shortly after we arrived in the city, our teacher told us we would be going on a field trip the following day so be sure to bring lunch with us. When we got home we told our mother, so she started cooking. She made some of our favorite foods, like stuffed cabbage. She put the food on a plate, covered it with another plate—like a lid—then tied a big towel at the four corners around the two plates. We proceeded to go to school and noticed all the other kids had brown paper bags with sandwiches in them. We looked at our food and we were too embarrassed to be seen with such a lunch, so we threw the whole thing in the garbage and didn't eat. It was better to go hungry than look like immigrants who didn't know what they were doing—we were just stupid kids and we hadn't realized yet we were immigrants who didn't know what we were doing and there was no shame in that.

Living on Leros, a person didn't have much need for long pants, shoes or coats. We had shoes, but we didn't want to ruin them, so we never wore them. When we arrived in NYC, we came with what we had—shorts and shirts. My father had no extra money to buy the things we needed. Someone started donating clothes and shoes to us and from then on, we had what we needed. At first, I wasn't able to wear shoes. The bottoms of my feet were so calloused from walking on rocks and thorns, I couldn't put them on.

I went to Patrick Henry Vocational School, studying a trade so I could work and support myself. I was learning how to put soles on shoes, how to make paper weights, and other types of carpentry. My brother, Steve, was working during the day and going to school at night. It was his dream to be an electronics engineer. I think it took him 15 to 20 years to get his degree. He was at Nasa and worked with the rocket program. We are all very proud of him. One brother and one sister became furriers, but they had to work for free to begin with. They were apprenticing. Everyone did what they had to do to help the family survive. All of us kids did what we had to do to help my parents provide for the family. That is what being a family is all about.

When I was in school, word was going around that I was a tough guy. I'm not sure how that started, but, it is what it is. A black guy challenged me to a fight. He came over to me and said, "I don't like you. I want to fight you."

I shrugged my shoulders. I didn't really want to fight but, everyone was already saying, "Fight! Fight!" so I went along with it. Our school was right next to Central Park so a lot of times we'd go there to eat our lunch. We set the fight for the same day at lunch time in Central Park. I figured he was going to beat the you know what out of me. I didn't know how to fight, and he was bigger than me and he was a boxer. I was pretty fast though, and I had learned how to use momentum to help me in all my chores on Leros. You get strong carrying two five-gallon buckets of water down a mountain.

We met up at the park and he took a swing at me. Instead of hitting me, he hit the air. I reached up and grabbed his arm and pulled him forward. He fell down by his own force. I fell on top of him and used my knees on his shoulders to hold him down then I started punching him like crazy. He managed to get up, so I grabbed his shirt and started hitting his chest with my head. Later, I learned I was using Jujitsu, but at the time, I was just trying to survive.

The bell rang and we all ran back to school. I was bleeding, so I went to see the nurse. She asked me what happened, so I told her I fell from a tree in the park. She just laughed and sent me back to my English class. My teacher asked me what happened, and I told her the same thing, I fell from a tree.

I was sitting at my desk, bandaged up, when someone knocked on the door. It was the same black man I had just fought in the park. He says, "I want to see this guy, the Greek." He walked to me and said, "I want to congratulate you. No one else would fight me. You were the only one." From that day on we became the best of friends and no one bothered us. When we walked by, everyone scattered.

I was never a smoker. Well, that isn't exactly true. I did try it—secretly. I didn't want my parents to find out. I began sneaking smokes when I was out with friends or wandering the city. At home, I'd go in the bathroom and shut the door, crack the window, and have a cigarette.

# Jimmy Proios

We lived in an L shaped house. One day when I was in the bathroom having a smoke, my father happened to be sitting in the living room and he saw smoke coming out of the bathroom window. He thought it was a fire. He ran to the bathroom and yelled, "Jimmy, is there a fire?"

I laughed and told him, "No, Dad, I just lit a piece of paper on fire cause it really stinks in here. I didn't want anyone dying because of me." I lied to my dad. From then on, I didn't smoke at home.

I did however, smoke on the subway platform. You couldn't smoke on the train, but I'd smoke until the train came. When the train would arrive, I'd put the cigarette out. One time I was waiting on the train, smoking, and I got really dizzy, I almost passed out. I made it to the bench before I fell and hit my head. I blamed it on smoking, so I took the whole pack and threw them in the garbage. I was done. I tried it again a few times, but I didn't really like it. I stopped for good when I went into the Navy.

# Chapter 8
# Growing Up

*"Day by day, what you choose, what you think and what you do is who you become."*
*Heraclitus, Philosopher of the 4th century BC*

At home, we were always hungry. My father didn't make enough money to feed us all. We ate once a day. When I turned 15, I knew something had to change. I quit school and found a job in a restaurant near my house. I didn't get paid anything. No money. But, I did get to take home little bits of leftover hamburger, ham, cheese, and bread. Sometimes, the boss would give me the end of a roast beef. I worked seven days a week, twelve hours a day. For food.

I would take whatever I got from working and put the food in the middle of the table and the whole family would just grab it and eat. Truman was president. There was no welfare. No food stamps. My uncle was supposed to be our sponsor, but it was hard for everyone. If we didn't have enough money, we didn't eat. You didn't go to the government to get your basic needs met like so many people do today. Things have changed, and not for the good.

I worked in that restaurant for a year and a half and I only worked for food for the table. When I'd gotten some experience, I started working for other restaurants—this time for money. But, I didn't make much, only $10 per week. At least I could help out at home. After a while, I found a job at a luncheonette owned by a couple of Jewish guys. I moved up in the world. I was making $20 a week. But, I worked. I mean, I really worked. Not only did they pay me better, but they paid me extra for every holiday—Jewish, Greek, and American! Every holiday there would be an envelope with a little extra money in it—a bonus. They even paid me extra for my name day. No, it's not my birthday. In Greece, we don't celebrate our birthdays, we celebrate our name days. What is a name day? Ah, I'll tell you.

In Greece, nearly every day of the year is named after a saint or a Christian martyr. When someone is named after one of these Christians, we celebrate them on the same day we celebrate the Saint's day. In Greece, back when I was young, people would come over, wish me a happy name day, and have something to drink, maybe a little to eat. It's not quite as popular today as it was back then, but it still happens.

So, October 26 is St. Dimitrious Day. My bosses gave me money—for my name day! I never had better bosses. I did work hard. No one ever had to tell me to keep busy, or to do my job. I took the initiative and really worked hard. If something was dirty, I cleaned it. If the trash needed taking out, I took it out. If the floor was cluttered, I swept. I even learned how to do some cooking. I was a grill man. I was making 45 dozen eggs every morning. Jews like to eat breakfast in restaurants. At least they did back then!

I loved working for my bosses. But, they were getting old and they retired so a new boss came in. I quit and went to work in the garment district. I worked with my mother, brother and sister as a furrier. I didn't like working in that job. The animal fur got into everything, my mouth, my lunch, you name it. I hated it.

We found a shack down on 27th Street, near 6th and 7th Avenue. It really was a shack. It wasn't a building. There were two separate shacks connected in the middle by a common wall and a parking lot behind the building. The guy who owned it was a friend of my father's. He said, "Paul, why don't you see if you can do something with this? If you succeed, you can give me something. If not, well, we tried."

We opened a small restaurant. My father, mother, brother, along with me, were working to see if we could make a living. We had rolls and coffee for five cents each. Another Greek opened another restaurant right next door to us, in a shack on the other side of our shack. Two Greek restaurants in two shacks, right next to one another. We just shrugged our shoulders. What could we do?

We weren't sure we were making any money, but at the end of the day when we counted what we'd brought in, we made $20 in one day—from food that cost a nickel.

Pretty soon we were making $35 a day. It was working. We were becoming successful.

My mother was cooking hamburgers, French fries, and things like this. I had worked at restaurants for a few years, so I knew what I was doing. My father on the other hand, didn't know squat about working in a restaurant. He had owned the tavern, of course, back on Leros, but he didn't do anything with the food preparation. That had been my mother's department.

One day a guy came in the restaurant and sat down at the counter. One of the items we sold was ice cream sandwiches. My father asked in broken English, "What would you like to have?"

He said, "I'll take an ice cream sandwich."

My father looked around, then asked, "What kind of bread would you like?"

They guy asked, "Bread?" I think because of my father's broken English he thought he misunderstood.

My dad asked, "Yes, what kind of bread do you want for the sandwich?"

I just watched this whole scene and listened to see what would happen next.

The guy gets a big grin on his face and said, "Rye."

My father scooped out three big scoops of ice cream and spread it on rye bread. He cut the sandwich in two, put it on a plate, and gave it to the guy. The guy busted out laughing. He thought it was the funniest thing he'd ever seen. Someone else walked in and the guy said, between laughing, "Hey, order an ice cream sandwich!"

My father said, "What's so funny?"

I stepped in to explain. "Dad, we already have pre-made ice cream sandwiches." I pointed them out to him, so he knew where they were.

One day, my brother and I were working in the restaurant, and a different guy came in and gave us a business card. He informed us he is our security company and our cost for security would be one dollar per day. I told him no, we couldn't afford to pay him a dollar a day. The next day we came into work and the whole front of the restaurant was torn off. It was all open. The guy who gave us the business card was standing across the street just watching us. When I looked at him he just shrugged. We started paying him one dollar a day. What else could we do?

The Greek guy, his name was George, running the restaurant next door came to my dad and said his lease was up. George says, "Paul, the owner isn't going to renew my lease. He wants to use the back lot for parking cars and he wants to tear down my space for more room. Why don't we work together, become partners and have one restaurant together?"

We were already doing well, what did we need a partner for? All of us, including my mother said, "Paul, we're making this work. This is our chance to make our restaurant grow. Even if they tear that side down, we can keep working here. We'll make it." My father refused. You would have thought he'd learned his lesson from what happened in Leros. But, my father wasn't that type of man. He always gave everyone the benefit of the doubt.

71

I was almost 18. I told my father, "You don't want to listen to my mother. You don't want to listen to my brother, or me. If you do this thing, then you don't need me."

I left and volunteered to join the Navy.

# Chapter 9
# The Navy

*"We must free ourselves of the hope that the sea will ever rest. We must learn to sail in high winds." Aristotle Onassis, Shipping magnate of the 20th century*

Since I was nearly 18, and the draft was going on, I chose to volunteer for the Navy. Two reasons, one, I didn't like to exercise and the guys in the Army and Marines had to do a lot more exercising than the guys in the Navy. And two, I wanted to be in the sixth fleet and go to Greece, specifically, to Leros.

When I went to sign up, the recruiter said, "You're not an American citizen. You can't join."

I had thought of myself as an American since coming to America. So, I said, "I'll become a citizen. I want to serve this country." Had my father said he had 7 children when he became a citizen, then we would have been citizens too just because he was approved. He didn't though, so I had to go through the process on my own.

He didn't speak very good English. Maybe they did ask him, and he didn't understand.

The recruiter asked me why I wanted to serve this country when I wasn't an American. I told him about seeing the United States flag when I returned from Palestine, and how much that flag meant to me. I think I made it clear how much I love this country because I convinced him.

He said, okay, so they gave me a test and I passed. I didn't even graduate from high school. Some other guys, ones born in this country, didn't pass.

After passing the test, I made the mistake of saying I died when I was a baby. I shouldn't have told them that story. They said I would be a liability. I insisted that I was fine and I'd never had another problem, so they ran all sorts of tests and such. They couldn't find anything wrong with me, so they said, okay, you can join.

Later on, the Navy dentist was looking at my teeth. I was having problems with my wisdom teeth. He offered to fix them, but I turned him down. After my experience when I was younger, and my two teeth were pulled, I kind of shied away from dentists. He did, however, get a good look at my teeth. He asked me if anything happened to me when I was younger. Did I have a disease or major sickness? I told him no, but I also told him about my dying when I was a baby. He told me he could tell something major had happened to me because my teeth in the back had turned a brownish color, as if they had started to die.

I went to boot camp in January in Bainbridge, Maryland. I was lying on my bunk looking out the window and I asked myself, "What the hell am I doing?" It was cold. There was snow on the ground. And I was far from my family. Boot camp was the hardest thing I've ever done. Not because of the exercise. Not because of having to take orders. But because, for the first time ever, I was away from my family. Family means everything to a Greek. More than anything, knowing how to adapt helped me get through boot camp. I knew how to blend in and be one of the guys.

I made it through boot camp and a new guy got assigned to the bunk under me. An ugly Irishman. Freckle faced, short, long nose, just ugly. I can say that because we became the best of friends.

One day he says, "Hey Jimmy, I'm Greek too."

I looked at him. "You? Greek? I don't believe it. You must be Irish!"

He said a few words in Greek and I raised my eyebrows. He wasn't fluent, but he knew some of the language. "Tell me your story."

He said, "My mother is Irish, but my father, he is Greek and he's from Leros."

"Leros? You have to be kidding me!" I was 13 when I left, and I didn't remember seeing him around the island or in school.

I called my mother and when I told her his last name, she says, "He's your cousin!" We got to be close after that. I went to visit his mother and father, in fact, his whole family, in Maryland.

In boot camp I was on flag duty. I had to raise the flag each and every morning and lower it each evening. We especially had to make sure the flag never touched the ground. The United States flag means so much to me. If I see anyone harming the flag, well, let's just say I might end up in jail.

I decided to learn how to work on diesel engines, mechanics, that sort of thing. Maybe the ship's engine on the way over from Leros sparked my interest to learn more about diesels.

During training, I was given the job of MP—military police. I was supposed to watch the chow room. The Navy had a rule. Take all you want but eat all you take. I took my job seriously. I wanted to do the very best I could in whatever I did.

Most of the time there was nothing going on but one day, a guy caught my eye as he moved through the line to get his food. I'm not sure what about him made me look, but, I did. He got a bowl of soup then he took a really big stack of crackers—the really big square ones, not the little ones you get today. He filled up his tray with his main meal then he sat down to eat.

He started eating his soup, but he didn't touch his crackers. Usually, the guys would crumble their crackers in the soup, but not this guy. He ate his main meal then he stood up and headed to the garbage bin. He was going to throw all those crackers away. He was ready to dump them when I reached him.

I asked, "What are you doing?"

He stopped what he was doing, holding the tray in his hand, he said, "I'm finished. So, I'm throwing my trash away."

I looked at the crackers then back to him, "Why did you take all those crackers? You didn't eat any."

He said, "Well, I guess it's just a habit. My mom used to give me crackers for my soup and I just took some because it reminded me of her."

I said, "Do you want me to report you?"

He looked surprised. "No."

Then you're going to go sit down and eat those crackers.

He took his tray, sat down and ate the crackers. No water, nothing. He started choking. I told him, "That's what you get. You shouldn't have taken them if you didn't plan on eating them. Next time only take what you're going to eat."

I think I was more aware of waste because I knew what it was like to be hungry and not have enough. I didn't like to see people waste food. I still don't.

After boot camp I was sent to Norfolk Virginia to work on a tugboat. I was on tugboat 59. We would guide the bigger ships into the docks. I got to know the cook pretty good. We called him, Cookie. Sometimes I would tell him to take the night off and I'd cook. The guys loved pastitsio—basically, Greek lasagna. They were crazy for it.

I learned the most English while I was in the navy. But, there were some words I still didn't know. We were standing outside on deck and Cookie had some love advice for me. He said, "Do you have a girlfriend?"

I said, "I might." I sometimes saw a girl, but I didn't really call her my girlfriend.

"Okay, well, if you want to make her really happy, you should tell her something."

"What should I tell her?"

"If you want to make her happy, tell her you've been castrated. She'll go crazy."

I asked him what it meant but he wouldn't tell me. He just told me to tell her. I knew he was up to no good. The next day I went to the library. I asked the librarian, "what does the word, castration, mean?"

She asked, "Why do you want to know that word?" I told her the story then she explained what the word meant.

The next day, I was on the tugboat and found Cookie standing on the edge of the boat. I said, "How are you doing, man? I just want to thank you for making that suggestion yesterday. When I told my girlfriend, she was so happy!"

He was surprised and said, "Really?"

I said, "Yeah." Then I shoved him in the water. I was on the tugboat for about 3 months.

After the tug boat 59 they transferred me to Yart oiler 59. I worked as a diesel mechanic. I was there for 3 months until my orders came through. Finally, I was transferred to aircraft carrier #59, the USS Forrestal. I was one day closer to visiting Leros.

I saw so many accidents on the ship. Planes that wouldn't take off fast enough would just drop in the water. Sometimes the catapult didn't work, or it would snap in two. One of the worst accidents I'd seen was when I was stationed in Guantanamo Bay. A sailor got hit with a plane and he was thrown into the water. The sharks finished him off in seconds. We were looking for what was left of him for three days and three nights. We couldn't find anything.

While we were in Cuba, when we'd have to go in the water, sailors in small boats would guard us with machine guns because there were so many sharks. You really had to move. The salt content in the water made it harder to swim. This all happened before my time with the Admiral.

When I had leave I would always go home. I'd call my mother and she would stop whatever she was doing to start preparing all my favorite foods. She would make stuffed cabbage rolls, stuffed peppers, and pastitsio. My brothers would sometimes get jealous and they would say, "Jimmy's coming home" when they saw mama cooking like crazy. But, I was the only one who went into the armed forces, so I was the only one who lived far from home. Or maybe it was because she loved me the most. I'm just kidding. She loved us all. But, I can think she loved me best.

On one leave, my sister, Irene, wanted me to go ice skating with her and a friend. The only problem was, I didn't know how to ice skate. On Leros, we didn't have ice. We didn't even get snow. I had strict instructions to wear my uniform. It was very important I had to come in uniform. I'm not sure why. Maybe it was because girls wanted to be seen with a guy in uniform.

Well, I met up with her and her friend, Annette, at the ice skating rink on 59th Street in Manhattan. I tried to stand up and immediately fell. Both girls came to help stand up and balance on the blade. My sister, Irene, was on one side of me and Annette was on the other side. They were holding me up, trying to teach me to ice skate. I wasn't very good at it. I was used to an ocean, not frozen water.

They took me around the rink and began to swing me around in circles. My legs were flying up and down—I was trying to keep my balance, but it didn't work. I fell. They were both laughing. I managed to crawl to the side of the ice rink and back to the bench where I took my skates off. I never tried to ice skate again.

My sister and Annette remained friends for a while. Then, Annette drifted away. Probably because she became famous. Maybe you've heard of her, Annette Funicello? Irene had wanted to be an actress, so she attended school at the Performing Arts Center in New York City. She met Annette and they became friends. Within a year, Annette auditioned to be on the Mickey Mouse Club and the rest is history.

There were times we were restricted from leaving the ship, maybe someone did something they weren't supposed to, or something happened on land and it was safer for us to remain on board. On one occasion, when we were restricted and all of us were on deck in formation, one of the sailors yelled out, "Give me liberty or give me death!" Everyone laughed.

I learned who Patrick Henry was that day. A founding father, and a governor of Virginia, he became famous through his speeches, including "Is life so dear, or peace so sweet, as to be purchased at the price of chains and slavery? Forbid it, Almighty God! I know not what course others may take; but as for me, give me liberty or give me death!" when he addressed the Second Virginia Convention. The captain made sure we knew who this man in America's history was.

I was never much of a drinker, not even in the Navy. I had a friend, well, I had more than one but one in particular. He was also very short. He made the height requirement to join the Navy by a quarter of an inch. He was really short. Sometimes in port I'd go out with him to nightclubs. When we were in London, we decided to go out to this beautiful nightclub.

There were English sailors. American sailors. Everyone was drinking and getting along just fine. My friend was drinking a lot. I should have known we were going to get into trouble. When he got drunk he got really happy. When he got really happy, he caused trouble. He looked at me with a big grin and said, "I want to fight."

I said, "John, please, sit down. We don't want to fight. We don't want to cause any trouble."

He said, "But, I want to fight." He wouldn't listen to me. I was afraid because I knew he was serious. I started for the door to leave as he was stepping up onto his chair. He yelled out across the night club, "I would like your attentions please." I was at the door by the time he said attention. I knew what was coming. He continued. "Ladies and gentlemen, I would like to say something. 'Eff' the Queen of England!"

The whole place erupted in a big fight. English sailors were fighting American sailors. Chandeliers were ripped from the ceiling. Mirrors were smashed and torn from walls. Dishes were broken. Walls were punched and had holes. Bottles of booze broken. Stains on the floor. Broken glass everywhere. The whole place was trashed.

The next day the Admiral called everybody to come up on deck. We were all standing at attention and we got reamed out. Then, every single sailor, whether you were at the night club or not, had to give $2.00 to send to the club so they could fix the place. 6000 sailors gave $2.00 each. We gave $12000 for the damage done. That was a lot of money back then. The nightclub was closed for 12 days so they could clean it up and fix everything. American sailors were banned from going back. Maybe the club started limiting how much alcohol they gave sailors from then on. You get enough alcohol in you and well, you'll do stuff you normally wouldn't.

John asked me later, "How come you didn't stay and help me fight?"

I told him, "If you had been in real danger, I would have come help. But, you didn't need me." I think seeing how alcohol makes people go crazy is one of the reasons I never drank very much.

One thing I noticed about the English is how cold they are. They're very stand-off-ish. We Greeks hug and kiss and are very demonstrative in giving affection. Their personalities match their weather. It's cold, gray and cloudy in England. While we were there it was sunny— the whole time. That alone was something of a miracle. Walking around I heard more than one person say, "Another day of sunshine? How many does that make now? Ten? I can't believe it!"

# Jimmy the Greek

In Scotland I asked for orange juice and they brought me hot juice, almost like tea. I guess that's the way they serve it there. I didn't ask for it again. I prefer my juice cold.

We were only in Italy for a couple of days and the thing I remember most about Portugal is how much it smelled like fish.

Of all the ports we docked at, Spain was my favorite. The people were so friendly. They were so humble. Many would approach us and talk to us, strangers. They would offer us something to drink, maybe something to eat. If we needed help with directions, they would show us where to go. I loved the people of Spain.

The country is just beautiful. The buildings and the architecture—it was so different than anything I'd seen on Leros or in America. In Leros, our buildings were simply made and in America, everything was modern and new. In Barcelona, there's a Catholic church, called "La Sagrada Familia Basilica", that is being built. It was started in 1883 and it's still being worked on today. They don't expect to finish it until 2026. That is crazy. The patience of the Spanish people—to know that generations of people will never see the building completed…yet they continue to believe and work, so their grandchildren or great grandchildren will see it—is incredible. That is believing in a dream and having a vision.

For J. Proice, FN, USN – with many best wishes – C.D Griffin, RAdm USNavy

# Chapter 10
# The Admiral

*"One of the most beautiful qualities of true friendship is to understand and to be understood." Seneca, philosopher, statesman, dramatist*

The USS Forrestal was named after the first secretary of defense, James Forrestal. The very first supercarrier, she was launched on December 11, of 1954. The ship was 1039 feet long and 252 feet wide. From keel to mast she equaled a 25-story building. I lived in a small city on the sea with 6000 other sailors.

The USS Forrestal was due to go to the Mediterranean 8 months after I was assigned. I was there for 2 to 3 months when an officer came and handed me a set of keys. He says, "There's a brand new 1957 Chevy down on the pier. You're going to be driving the Admiral."

I looked at him in disbelief. "Are you sure you want me? I'm not qualified." He didn't care. Qualified or not, I was driving the Admiral.

I had no idea who the Admiral was. I was shaking—nervous. I didn't know what to do. I found the car, got everything ready, and waited. Finally, I saw the Admiral. He was a huge man. I opened the door for him, he climbed in the back seat, then I closed the door and went to the driver's seat. I had my orders. I knew where I was going—I had directions. We were in Norfolk Virginia. Yet, I was so nervous, I was unable to do anything.

Sweat was running down my face and into my eyes. My hands were clammy. He watched me try to get the car into first, then second, then third gear, grinding the gears as I went. Every time I started to press the gas pedal, the car would stall. I was watching him watch me through the rear-view mirror.

Finally, he tapped me on the shoulder and said, "Sailor?"

Shaking, I said, "Yes, Sir?"

He asked, "What is your name?"

I answered, "James Proios, Sir." I pronounced my last name syllable by syllable.

"What kind of name is that?"

I said, "Greek."

He said, "Greek, stop the car."

I wanted to mention that we hadn't gone anywhere yet, but, instead I just listened.

He continued, "I'm about to give you an order."

I thought, Oh crap! He's big. He's going to kill me.

He asks, "Do you go to the bathroom?"

That was an easy question. I said, "Yes, Sir."

"I want you to tell me in detail what you do when you go to the bathroom. Don't leave anything out."

"Sir?"

"Sailor, did you hear me? I said, in detail, that's an order."

"Yes, Sir." I shakily started out, telling him, in detail what I had to do to go to the bathroom. He wanted a full description of both kinds of bathroom trips. I went through the whole procedure, from unzipping and unbuttoning to wiping. I had no idea where this was going but when I finished, I looked at him, fully expecting to be relieved of my duties and put on kitchen detail.

He said, "You know something, Greek? I do the same eff'n thing. I get up like you. I take a shower like you. I put on my pants like you. I shave like you."

He went on in detail describing how he was a man, just like me. I felt better.

He said, "Okay, shall we go? You have good directions and everything?"

I told him I did.

He said, "Well, let's get going. We're late."

We were on a long pier. I was going about 15 miles per hour. He says, "Greek, we have gas?"

I said, "Yes, Sir."

He said, "Step on it, man. We're late."

I got the car up to speed and managed to get him to where he was going. When we got there, he told me I could do what I wanted as long as I was back in an hour. An hour later, I was there waiting for him. Then I took him to an Embassy party. He got so drunk that night, he passed out and I had to drag him back to the car. He slept the entire ride back to the ship.

When I got there, I realized I had a problem. There's a long plank you have to walk up to board the ship. I left the Admiral in the car and decided to go upstairs first to talk to the officers. I asked them to make themselves scarce. I didn't want to cause a scene. At first, they said no. They weren't going to listen to a lowly sailor. I then told them I had to bring the admiral up through the officer's hall and I didn't want them to see him because he was drunk.

Finally, they understood so they left the room for about ten minutes—just enough time for me to get him up the ramp and into his bedroom. I helped him undress then helped him into bed. I didn't feel right leaving him, so I stayed in a chair in his room all night in case he needed me.

When he woke up he asked, "What are you doing here? Why are you looking at me like that?"

I told him I got him safely back to his room and no one saw him. When he realized what I'd done, how I protected him from being seen by everyone and watching over him that night, he couldn't believe it. He wanted his breakfast, so he called his Filipino cook to make his food. I started to leave, and he asked me where I was going. I told him, I was going to the mess hall to get some breakfast. He said, no, Greek. You're going to eat right here with me. The remainder of my time in the Navy was serving the Admiral. To think what could have been a really bad situation with me ending up peeling potatoes for 6000 men turned into the best job a guy could have.

The Admiral ended up being a great friend. He was my boss, yes, but also a friend. He trusted me. He knew I'd be there to have his back. I learned he'd have mine too.

The USS Forrestal was based in Italy for six months. We went to Portugal, England, Spain, and Scotland. It seemed we went everywhere but Greece. Finally, I asked him why we hadn't gone to Greece yet.

He told me we weren't going because The United States sided with Britain in planning Cyprus' re-unification with Turkey, which the people of Cyprus were against. They wanted their independence and if that couldn't happen, they wanted to be re-united with Greece. Since the United States agreed with Great Britain, American soldiers were being blamed and beaten up when they were off base in Greece. So, they decided to skip Greece. I was so upset. I told him I joined the Navy so I could go to Greece. He told me to take it easy and not worry about it.

The Admiral told me I was taking a 15 day leave and I was going to Leros.

"How am I going to get there?"

He said, "What are you worried about? I'll take care of everything. Just get your stuff packed and ready."

The next thing I knew I was in a car headed for the airport where I boarded an American transport plane headed to Turkey. It wasn't first class. It wasn't even coach, but I was on my way to Greece. The plane was enormous. Besides me, there were two tanks and three or four Jeeps to keep me company. I questioned whether the plane would be able to lift off with all that weight, but, it did. Thousands of pounds just flying through the air—a modern marvel.

I started to learn to play music when I was in the Navy. I began with the mandolin. When we were stationed in Italy, I was filmed for television when I was playing with my dad and a group of other musicians. Not that I was that good, but I got to play. My mother's brother was there. He was an Italian policeman—a carabinieri. Sometimes I would stay at his house since we were in Italy so long.

Not every Greek understood the Admiral's humor. When docking was not possible, the Admiral and I would use a smaller boat to tender. Occasionally, I would come to shore before him to get the car ready. One particular time, I was standing on the pier talking to my uncle when the Admiral arrived from the ship. He walked up to us and asked, "Hey Greek, who is this clown?"

"Admiral, Sir, this is my uncle." My uncle was so insulted. To help show he was just kidding, the Admiral invited the whole family back to the ship for dinner.

Mostly, I drove the Admiral, but there were times I would drive him, his wife, and his daughter. One day we were all four in the car and I farted. It was one of those silent but deadly farts. One that could cause a person to pass out. I was good. I didn't even crack a smile. His daughter was in the front seat and I was hoping she wasn't going to throw up. The Admiral and his wife were in the back seat.

# Jimmy the Greek

Next thing I know, the Admiral's wife was hitting him. No one said a word. I cracked the window a little, so we could get some fresh air. Once we got to his house he took his wife and daughter into the house then he came back. "You eff'n Greek. You farted, and my wife blamed me." We had a lot of fun together.

When we were at sea there were times I had absolutely nothing to do. My job was to serve the Admiral and if he didn't need me, well, I was pretty much free to do what I wanted. Except sleep. I couldn't take a nap. And wouldn't you know it, taking a nap is what I wanted to do. On deck there was a large area of sacks, large bags used for rice and potatoes. I couldn't go sleep in my bunk, so I'd crawl up in those sacks and hideout and sleep.

Normally, I wasn't needed but this particular day we were at what is called a "friendly war" with other ships and submarines. This time I slept through the PA system calling out, "Jimmy the Greek, you're needed on the bridge. Jimmy the Greek, please report to the bridge."

A friend of mine heard, knew where I was, and came to get me. Once I got the sleep out of my eyes and the drool off my cheek, I hurried to the bridge. When I got there, I heard Greek music playing.

My commander motioned toward a chair. "Sit down and listen."

I heard the enemy talking in Greek. A submarine in our little friendly war was trying to out maneuver us by talking in Greek. They had no idea The USS Forrestal had one Greek on the ship. They torpedoed us, with duds of course, but, if the duds hit us we were out of the game, we would lose. I listened to their plans and told everyone on the bridge what they were saying.

The captain was able to dodge both torpedoes. One passed us on the left, one on the right. They couldn't believe they missed us and were talking in Greek, so, I answered in Greek.

"You think you have all the Greeks, but you don't. We have one Greek in 6000 sailors—Jimmy the Greek!" We all laughed.

The Admiral was married with one daughter, no sons. At that time, the Naval Academy in Annapolis, Maryland only accepted men. I had become the son the Admiral never had. We joked with one another. Swore at one another. We were comfortable together and we trusted each other.

He taught me to believe in myself, that I could do whatever I set my mind to. I was not better than, but just as good as everyone else. I loved him, I loved him like a father.

The Admiral approached me and asked me if I'd like to go to the Naval Academy to become an officer. He begged me to stay in the Navy then retire after 20 years. I argued with him, I didn't have a diploma. I didn't finish school. I used whatever excuse I could find. He told me he'd take care of it. I might have to go a little longer, but I'd get my diploma and an education, and I could become an officer. One of the dumbest things I've ever done in life is not take him up on his offer. I was young and stupid, and I made some bad decisions.

I looked at him and said, "I'm going to fill up that sea bag and I'm going to walk to New York City. I won't be in the Navy anymore. It's time to go home."

He said, "You stupid Greek. If you change your mind, you tell me."

I changed my mind, but I was much older, and it was too late.

I was honorably discharged while in Norfolk, Virginia. After I got out of the Navy I kept thinking about what the Admiral had said to me, that I could go back. When I was nearing the one-year mark of being out of the Navy, I received a letter offing me ten thousand dollars to re-enlist. They figure they're saving all the money it takes to train soldiers if the Navy can get those discharged to come back. I still didn't do it. It is the one thing I truly regret.

# Chapter 11
# Visiting Leros

*"The whole life of a man is but a point in time;
let us enjoy it." Plutarch, Greek historian,
biographer, and essayist*

I wanted to go to Piraeus, a Greek city by the shore, because I had some friends there. I was in my United States Navy Uniform and I only had American dollars. I tried to buy a train ticket but the guy working the booth wouldn't serve me. He said they didn't take American dollars. I walked away, not sure what to do.

A guy approached me and said, "Hey, Joe, how are you?" If someone in Greece don't know your name, they call you Joe. Everyone's a Joe. He said, "What are you doing here?" He was surprised to see a sailor.

I told him "go to hell" in Greek.

He said, "Are you Greek, man?"

"Yeah, I'm Greek." Then I told him the story about the ticket. He took the dollar and he left. I thought, great, there goes my money. Ten minutes later he returned and handed me 30 drachmas—silver Greek coins (before the introduction of the Euro). "Wow, that's a lot of money. I thought you were going to rob me."

He said, "No, I wasn't going to rob you. I just wanted to help you."

I thanked him and gave him 10 of the drachmas for his help. He couldn't believe I was giving him so much money. The American dollar was worth a lot of Greek money. He nearly dropped to kiss my feet.

I got back in line to buy a ticket and the guy never gave me my change. Maybe he thought I wouldn't notice the difference. He still didn't know I was Greek. At least I got a train ticket.

The train wasn't in the station yet, so I stood around, impatiently waiting. Three Greek soldiers approached me and said, "Dimitri?"

It took me a minute, but I remembered who they were. When I was in Norfolk, Virginia, these same soldiers came to our base to pick up four destroyers and two submarines. Because I spoke Greek, I was in charge of seeing to them and making sure communication was right. I had to change the signs on the destroyers and subs from English to Greek—make sure they were done correctly. These guys ended up staying on base for five days.

One morning, around breakfast time, I went down to see them, and they practically had nothing to eat. A cup of tea, a couple pieces of toast, a little butter and a few olives. I asked them, where are your eggs and bacon? Everyone else at base was having a good breakfast of eggs, bacon, sausage, potatoes, toast…and even more if they wanted it. These guys weren't being treated right. I was getting angry.

That night I went down to see them at supper and the same thing. The United States sailors were having steak and potatoes, but the Greek soldiers had a dried-out piece of chicken, a slice of bread and some rice. I got mad!

I went upstairs and talked to the captain of the ship. "Do you want me to report you?" He made a bunch of excuses, trying to tell me they weren't supposed to be eating like the other sailors, but I wouldn't listen. I told him I was going to talk to the Admiral. He begged me not to. The next morning, I went down to see the Greek sailors and they were feasting. They were so thankful. They recognized me right away when they saw me waiting for the train in Piraeus and thanked me again for helping them. I hate to see anyone go without food. It reminds me of the many times I was hungry and had nothing.

On Leros, the first thing I did was drop and kiss the ground. I love Leros. Don't get me wrong, I love America more, but Leros was where I was born. It was where I ran and played as a boy and most of my childhood memories all came from those mountains and those beaches.

While on Leros, I stayed with my aunt. The next morning, I went out to the town square to see who was around, so I wore some of my cousin's clothes, civvies, that were around my size. It was early morning and I was wandering around the square, drinking coffee, talking to friends I hadn't seen in a long time. Just enjoying being home and seeing everyone. Leros is a small island and most everyone knows everyone else. You can't help but know most everyone.

All of a sudden, the Greek Military Police parked a Jeep near us and approached us. "Are you Mr. James Proios? Dimitrious Proios?"

I told the officer asking, "Yes."

He said, "You're under arrest."

I had no idea why I'd be under arrest but agreed to go with them. I didn't do anything and besides, I was an American Citizen. It took us about five minutes to get to the Police Station. I was put in a room with a big guy, like an admiral but even more important. I was waiting for him to say what he wanted with me and suddenly, he started cursing at me. I lost my temper and started saying the same things back to him in Greek, not English.

He says, "You're talking to me like this?" His face was turning red in anger. I'm sure there were no Greek soldiers who dared to speak to him this way.

He called for the guards to put me in jail and I said, "Stop. Are you a judge?" It was then I realized why he was having me arrested. In the Greek Navy, sailors had to wear their uniforms at all times, even when off duty or on leave. Someone squealed on me, that I was in the Navy and out of uniform.

He said, "Don't you recognize me? I'm a captain."

I told him, "No. I don't know you. Do me a favor, sit down at your desk." He started to protest, how dare I tell him, a captain, to sit down at his desk. Once again, I told him to just sit down. I took out my wallet and put my ID in front of him. He looked at it, then he looked at me.

"You're in the American Navy? I thought you were in the Greek Navy? You were in your civvies…and I thought…"

"No, I'm in the American Navy. I'm an American citizen."

His face turned red and he was obviously angry and probably embarrassed. He stuttered a little then he asked the guard to go find the guy who squealed on me. I stopped him. "Hey, wait a minute. Just leave it alone. Let's introduce ourselves." We started over and introduced ourselves. We talked for a while and I invited him to go with me to get something to eat. At the time, I was earning $156.00 a month and he was earning $12.00 a month. I bought his dinner. He was thankful.

# Chapter 12
# NYC: On leave and After the Navy

*"Music is a moral law. It gives soul to the universe, wings to the mind, flight to the imagination, and charm and gaiety to life and to everything." Plato, Philosopher of the 5th century*

I really started concentrating on learning to play music once I left the Navy. My brother was learning the bouzouki, a long neck wooden instrument with a round body, similar to a lute, and played like a guitar. I would just sit and listen to him and watch him play. He read music, but it looked like a bunch of chicken scratches to me. When I picked up his bouzouki and started playing, he was very surprised. I played by ear, not by reading music.

I started getting requests from friends, "Why don't you start an orchestra?" I recruited a drummer, then a guitarist and an organ player. We would play every weekend. At first, other Greeks played with me. But, many times they wouldn't show up for gigs and I would be without a drummer or a guitar player, so I started hiring Jewish musicians. They always showed up. I never wondered if we'd be short a player.

At one wedding, an Italian wedding, 500 people attended. I received a thousand kisses that night. Stella was at this wedding too. This was after we were married. The people loved our music. I received so many job offers, so many people called me to play for them I had to turn some down. I just didn't have enough days in the week. Most of these people missed Greece and our music reminded them of home, a bit of nostalgia. I would play longer than I was supposed to because I enjoyed playing, and the people didn't want to go home.

If musicians were bad, the people would throw eggs at them. I guess maybe I am a musician because I never experienced being covered with raw eggs.

If there is one thing I wish my grandson would know it would be to learn to play some instrument—learn to make music. Music brings such joy and happiness to people's lives. Even in the worst of times, music can put a smile on someone's face.

If you've paid attention to musicians, a lot of them drink and smoke. I wasn't ever into either, not even when I was in the navy. And with Greek musicians, the odds are even higher. In fact, 40% of Greeks over the age of 15 smoke. I don't know why. I just remember the time I got sick waiting for the train and I wasn't interested in smoking after that. When people learn I'm Greek and I don't smoke, they can't believe it.

I remember one wedding my orchestra was hired to play for. It was a very odd job. We were setting up and the man who hired us came to me and said, "I'm the one who signed the contract. I'm the one who hired you so I'm the one who is going to pay you. You need to do what I tell you to do." The room was empty. No one was there yet. The bride and groom were still on their way from the church. He said, "I want you to pick one tune and play it over and over again. I don't care which song it is. Don't play anything else."

I said, "Are we going to be playing all night?"

He said "Yes, just play that one song. Nothing else."

What could we do? He hired us. He was going to pay us. We had to do what he said. So, we started playing a Greek song over and over. People started coming and sitting down and people started to notice we were only playing one song. They were like, what the hell is going on?

People began approaching us and asking us if we knew any other songs. We just told them yes and kept playing the one song. I told them if they wanted to hear something different, they had to talk to the guy who hired us. Then I pointed him out, but I kept playing that one Greek song, again and again.

One guy must have talked to the father because he let us play one song the guy requested then we had to go back to the original Greek song we had been playing all night. It was so boring!

We normally played at a wedding for five hours. This one lasted only two hours. Everyone was so tired of that song, they left. They didn't want to hear it any more. We figured he must have hated the groom or maybe the groom's parents, but he didn't want the ceremony lasting very long. He paid us, and he gave us a good tip too. By the time we left I was sick of playing that song. But, I guess his plan worked. The night ended early.

At another wedding the bride was sitting in the chair and the groom was removing the garter. The photographer was there waiting for the moment the garter came off, so he could take the picture. The groom was supposed to remove the garter then throw it. He wouldn't do what he was supposed to do, instead, he kept his hands on her leg, rubbing his bride's knee. She got so mad she stood up and kicked him and left. They just got married. He laughed then he spent the rest of the night dancing with their guests. The bride was gone. She didn't come back. I have to wonder how that marriage turned out.

I had my most embarrassing moment at a wedding. Everyone was there. The guests were seated. The bride and groom, the best man, and the maid of honor were all sitting together. I had just bought a brand new cordless microphone. I bought it to show off—I paid $700 for it. That was a lot of money at the time.

I walked to the wedding party and asked the best man if he would say a few words then I handed him the microphone. He looked at me and he very seriously said, "I'm not the best man. I'm the groom."

I was confused. The groom was quite old, and the bride was very young. The young man I thought was the groom was actually the best man. I was so embarrassed. I turned as red as the sauce on Stella's spaghetti! Everyone at the wedding was listening and I had no idea I had the wrong man.

My first car was a 1955 Chevrolet. I bought it for $500 from a guy in Brooklyn. Well, Steve is the one who found the car. I had to drive it with my feet propped up on both sides because the salt and snow ate a hole clean through the floorboard. If I didn't watch what I was doing, my foot would slip through the hole. I finally screwed a metal plate to the floor, so my foot wouldn't go through any more. At one time I owned five cars and not one of them ran.

Then I bought a 1961 Renault. The engine was on the back and you had to start the car with a crank. It was easier to start it if the car was on a bit of a hill. I could give it a little push then put it in gear and pop the clutch. This was in 1964. My brother-in-law was with me and we parked at the top of a hill near where we were going. When we came back to get the car, it wouldn't start. I tried to turn the wheel and it wouldn't turn. The wheel was locked in place. We got out and kicked the tires to release the steering wheel. Still nothing. The steering wheel wouldn't turn. I had no idea what was going on. We had to call a wrecker and pay $7 to have the car towed to a shop. $7 was a lot of money.

The guy came to pick us up and asked us what was wrong with it. I told him I didn't know. The three of us picked up the car and turned it around so he could hoist it, it was a small, lightweight, car. All three of us went to the shop with my car being towed. When we got to the shop he said, "give me the keys." He put the keys in the car then the steering wheel unlocked. I just shook my head. I had never seen that before. I didn't try unlocking the steering wheel when the keys were in the ignition. They had been in my pocket the whole time.

# Chapter 13
# Stella

*"By all means, get married: if you find a good wife, you'll be happy; if not, you'll become a philosopher." Socrates, Philosopher of the 5th century BC*

The entire 15 days I spent in Leros, mothers were bringing their daughters to see me, hoping to marry them off to me. I met them, but nothing happened. I wasn't interested. I just enjoyed being back on Leros and seeing friends and family.

Stella's brother married my cousin, the daughter of my uncle who owned the grocery store in Leros. When I was on leave from the Navy, and I visited for those 15 days, I went to my cousin's house and I just walked in. Stella was there watching their baby. She got scared when she turned around and she thought her brother had come in and purposefully scared her. She started to curse then she saw it was me and she stopped and apologized.

That was the first time I saw Stella after we were grown up. I had played with her at school when we were little. She had been a neighbor. Her father cut my hair. Yet, I never really saw her until we were adults. Even then, I wasn't planning on getting married. I was young. I was in the navy. And marriage was the last thing on my mind.

When I was growing up on Leros, there was a couple around my parents' age who lived next door to us. They had no children of their own, but they enjoyed spending time with us. She used to make us stuffed cabbage and we used to call her mother because she was like a second mother to us. When I visited Leros, this couple invited me to come and eat with them. She made me stuffed cabbage since I loved it so much as a boy. After dinner, he took me aside asking his wife to leave us alone. He pointed next door, to where Stella had lived, and he said, the person you marry should be her, meaning Stella. She is the right one for you.

I was polite and said the right things, but again, I wasn't looking for a wife. I finished my visit and left for the ship.

When I was in Italy, I bought some cards and sent one to everyone I had visited with—my cousins, aunt, friends, and of course Stella. Stella was the only person who answered my letter. We started writing to each other. That is how we began courting.

For three years we wrote each other. I would receive her letters on the ship and I'd head to the deck to read them. One time, it was so windy the letter blew out of my hand and into the ocean before I could read a word. I wrote her back and let her know I didn't get to read the last letter she sent. Turns out, Stella kept a copy of her letters, so she sent me another copy.

I proposed in a letter. Really, I made a statement that I was going to come to Leros to marry her. She said yes, she would like to marry me, in her next letter. She had been taking care of her brothers and sisters. Her mother had died, and she was like a mother and a father to her younger brothers and sisters. She was the oldest. Her father was still alive, but back then a man didn't take care of the children. He would give her part of his paycheck each week and she would take care of everything at the house. He would spend the rest of the money at the tavern. By agreeing to marry me, she was passing the responsibility of their younger brothers and sisters to her sister, Koula.

After the Navy I really hadn't considered getting married yet. I was writing letters back and forth with Stella, and I planned on marrying her someday, but, I was enjoying life and didn't really think about getting married at that time. I knew I would in the future, but, I was young, and I didn't mind waiting. My parents are the ones who made me think about getting married. They are the ones who pushed me in that direction—back to Leros.

Parents have a way of influencing our decisions. They have lived a little longer than we have and deserve to at least be heard.

I got out of the Navy and was working but not making much. I wanted to go to Leros and marry Stella, but, I didn't have the money to travel. My mother realized what was going on and talked to my father. He said to me, "are you going to marry her or not?" The Greeks have a saying, "Either get married early, or become a monk early." Since I had no intention of becoming a monk, I got married early.

He loaned me eight hundred dollars, so I could travel to Leros to get married. My sister, Irene, gave me her wedding dress, so Stella would have an American gown to wear. We were the first ones to get married American style in Leros. We still had some of the Greek traditions, but I was an American and Stella was about to become an American. We had to have something from America.

I went to Greece and four days later, we got married at the church right above the house where Stella grew up. My father-in-law took off work the four days between when I arrived until we got married so he could act as our chaperone. He was afraid I might attack Stella or something. But, I wouldn't do that. When I was a young boy I asked my mother where babies came from. She didn't want to talk to me about sex, so she told me from the knee. I grew up thinking babies came out of the knee. Even when I was 13, she was still saying babies came from the knee. So, why would I attack Stella? He had nothing to worry about. I wasn't interested in her knee.

I married Stella on July 18, 1962. Of course, I insist she got married and not me. If you think about it, it makes sense. She changed her name to Proios. I didn't change my name. So, who got married? Stella got married. That's who!

# Jimmy the Greek

There's a tradition in Greek weddings that the bride and groom are supposed to step on each other's toes during the ceremony. Whoever manages to step on the other's toes first, will supposedly have the upper hand in their relationship. Of course, every Greek man wants to be the boss of the family—the king of his house. All the guys at the wedding were all saying, Jimmy, step on her, hurry, step on her. I didn't know what they meant. They wanted me to step on her? So, Stella heard everyone telling me to step on her, so she stepped on my toes instead. Everyone laughed. She made it clear who was going to be the boss in our family. Maybe it was me who got married that day!

Stella says she married me because I was a tall, handsome man. I was in the Navy and she loves a man in uniform. But mostly because I was an American by then. She didn't want to marry anyone on Leros. She didn't want to stay on the island.

The wedding reception was a great big party. In Leros, musicians play for weddings by taking turns. If they get a chance to play, then they get paid. People throw money at the musicians while they're playing. When orchestras or bands learn there is a wedding reception going to happen, you'll see them hanging around outside waiting for a turn. At our wedding we had so many family members who were musicians, the bands lining up outside didn't get to play. My cousins got into a fight with a band who was waiting to play. They don't even have to be invited, they just show up.

After the wedding we went to Athens to the American Embassy and filled out the paperwork for Stella to come to the United States. Three months later, Stella joined me in New York City. We started petitioning right away for Stella's sisters and brothers to come to the United States. It took us four years to bring them to New York. The day they flew out, I'll never forget. It was April 21, 1967. At the very same time the plane was taking off and, in the air, a group of military colonels were initiating a coup in Greece. The exact same day. Had the plane been scheduled to leave later in the day, they wouldn't have been able to come, who knows for how long. The dictatorship lasted for seven years and the people of Greece were subjected to extremely hard times, including torture of those suspected of being communists or political opponents. Freedom of the press and freedom of thought were taken away. All the freedoms the Greek people had enjoyed for years, was suddenly taken away. Yes, it is clear that had that plane not taken off early that morning, before the coup, Stella's family wouldn't have been able to come for quite a while.

None of my brothers or sisters, or my mother or father were able to come to our wedding. There were, however, cousins and many friends who came and celebrated with us.

Stella's mom died when she was just 42. Stella took over raising her sisters and brothers and taking care of the cooking, cleaning, laundry and shopping. She had eight sisters and brothers and naturally, she was very close to them since she helped raise them. After she came to New

York City to be with me, her younger sister, Koula, took over the job as caretaker.

All but her brother was able to come. I made a trip back to Greece to help him get permission to leave. His Visa wasn't going through. I went to the American Embassy and I told them I was an American citizen, I served in the US Navy—I served my country and was honorably discharged—and I wanted my brother-in-law to come back to America with me. I had proof, in writing, of everything I told him. Ten minutes later I was sitting in front of the Ambassador. He asked me to tell him what was going on, so I told the story again.

Even when you have the Ambassador on your side, you normally don't get results right away. It could take a month or two to get the travel visas. Not this time. He asked, "When are you leaving?" I told him, "In a few days." He replied, "You can take him with you." Just like that he approved my brother in law's visa.

This brother is the one who ended up working with the Italians in New York City—in construction. He might have been affiliated with the mob. But just a little bit. His wife was going to go with us on our last trip to Leros, but she had to have knee surgery. Maybe she can go next year.

If you ask me if I think I'm romantic, I would say yes. If you ask Stella, if she thinks I'm romantic, she'll say no. I come in, I give her a kiss. Give her a little hug. To me, that is romance. For her, romance is flowers, and remembering her birthday (and not giving her flowers the day after she reminds me it's her birthday). I guess our definition of romance isn't the same.

# Jimmy Proios

Stella and I have been married 55 years. We've had our problems. Neither one of us is perfect. But, we're perfect for each other. I've never been in love with any other woman. There is only Stella. I think that might be as romantic as I get.

# Chapter 14
# New York: Early
# Married Life

*"Raising children is an uncertain thing; success
is reached only after a life of battle and worry."*
*Democritus, Philosopher from the $5^{th}$ century*

We bought a house in Queens Village. And when I say we bought a house, think of the movie "My Big Fat Greek Wedding" and all the family involved in one another's business. My brother, my sister, myself—we paid $18,000.00 for a basement and two floors. To buy that same house today would be over a million dollars—maybe more. When Stella arrived, she weighed 98 pounds soaking wet, that's how skinny she was.

My mother was there too, and she and Stella grew very close. In 1964, my mother became sick. They took her to the hospital because they thought she had gallstones. The doctors performed surgery, but they closed her back up.

Yes, she did have gallstones, but she also had liver cancer. Within one month, she died. She is buried in New York and when we travel, we go visit her grave.

The person I admire most in this world was my mother. She was strong. She never complained. She did what had to be done. She was always there for us kids. She went through hell and she continued to love us and care for us. She was the least selfish person I have ever known. I admired my father too, but, it was different with him. He was coming and going. When I was young, fathers weren't expected to help raise the kids. They were supposed to earn a living and support their family. The women raised the children and took care of the house.

My mother showed her love for us through her cooking. She was chubby…she loved her own cooking too. She was beautiful. Inside and out.

I placed my mother on a pedestal. She is the one who taught me to love, to work, to give everything for those I love. She was still alive when our daughter, Sophia, was born but not our son, Peter. Before she died I was sitting with her. She was very sick. I asked, "Mom, how do you feel?"

She turned her head to look at me and answered, "You don't think I recognize you, do you?"

I said, "No, Mom, that's not what I said. I asked you how you feel." She was right, though. I was testing her to see if she recognized me, if she was still with us enough to remember me. She knew me well enough to know exactly what I wanted. I needed to know she still knew me, that she was still there with me.

She told me, "I know exactly who you are."

I was glad. She stayed with us mentally until the very end.

When I was younger, I wanted to be a priest. When my mother died, I was no longer sure there was a God. I became a seeker instead of a believer. I was so angry at him. I shook my fist at the sky and said, "it isn't fair! If you exist, why didn't you do something?" I wanted God to prove to me he was there. I wanted him to kick the door down and punch me, slap me, throw me from one side of the room to the other. I wanted to see the miraculous. I wanted him to show me he existed. I still do today. If he does, then I will be the most faithful believer of them all. I take the Greek saying, "The saint who works no miracles isn't glorified," literally. When I see it, I'll be faithful. Until then, I'm still seeking.

Stella, on the other hand has a strong faith. She prays for the whole world, but I'm pretty sure she prays extra hard for me.

I met Stella's mother when I was younger, but I didn't really know her, not like I would have if she had been alive when Stella and I married. I know she was a good woman, just like my mother, because she raised Stella. You can tell a lot about people by looking at their children, especially mothers.

My daughter was born the same year as my mother died, 1964. We named her for my mother, Sophia. I wanted to name her after my wife's mother, Irene, but Stella insisted we name her Sophia. She loved my mother and she wanted to honor her. My son was born five years later, and we named him Peter, after my uncle, the one who adopted my sister, Irene. My father had already had many grandchildren named after him, so we thought we would give my uncle a namesake. My uncle was also Peter's Godfather. I didn't want a big family, which is not normal for us Greeks, but that's okay. We had two children and we were happy.

Sophia was always strong willed. Every time we would go into the store, she would ask for something. A piece of bubble gum or candy. A toy. She would see something and want it. Sometimes we'd have to say no. Sometimes because we didn't have the money and sometimes because she didn't need to have it. She would get so angry when we would say no. Look at her now. She goes after what she wants. Being stubborn isn't always a bad thing.

Peter was different. At some point he had asked for a toy and I told him, "We don't have the money right now. Maybe next time." The following time we took him to the store he started pointing at something he wanted and repeated what I told him, "maybe next time." It became his line every time we went into a store when he was a small child.

Sophia was kicking and screaming and mopping the floors because she didn't get what she wanted. Peter refused to ask for anything. Every child is different.

When I was young, my father was distant with us. It wasn't popular back then to be emotional with your children. A father was supposed to provide for their family, make sure they were safe, and discipline the children. The mother was the one who handed out hugs and fixed scrapes and wiped away tears. Even then, she didn't have a lot of time for nonsense because life was hard, and she expected us kids to be tough.

When I was a young father, my kids expected me to hug them and be with them, spend time with them. I worked long hours and Sophia didn't like it. One day I had finished work at the restaurant and was going to play for a music gig, so I called home to talk to Stella. Sophia answered the phone instead and wanted to know where I was. She asked, "Why are you going to work?" I told her "to make money." She then said, "Look in your pocket. You have money!" She was only four or five and she had no concept of how much money it took to provide. All she knew is she wanted me home more.

It wasn't easy. We were still struggling to find our way in the land where dreams come true. I went back to what I knew, working in restaurants.

I was so good at my job, I remembered each customer and what they wanted for breakfast. When I saw them come in, I'd start preparing their food. I worked hard 6 days a week. I worked in the restaurant six days then on weekends after I left the restaurant, I played music for weddings, bar mitzvahs, birthday parties, and any other celebration. I would get home at 1 or 2 in the morning then have to be back at the restaurant at 5 am to open the place up for breakfast. Mondays were my day off. I slept all day long. I worked this way for five years.

At the restaurant there were large coffee urns. As you might guess, we went through a lot of coffee in the morning for breakfast. Once we were finished with one urn, we'd get more coffee started right away before moving to the next urn. If not, we'd run out of coffee and our customers wouldn't be too happy.

I toasted a corn muffin and put it and some butter on a plate. I did this every day. I could do it with my eyes closed. When the cook started the new urn of coffee, he accidently left the spout open and water soaked the muffin.

He started yelling and screaming at me. I told him, "I can make another one. It's not a big deal." But, he kept yelling at me.

Something in me snapped. I don't know if I was getting tired of doing the same job over and over or if I'd just had a hard morning and was finished. I've never walked away from any job in my life, except this one. When he wouldn't stop yelling, I went to the kitchen to the main boss and told him he was going to have to cover my job because I was leaving. I took my apron off and put it on his desk then I left. I just walked out. I wasn't going to take being yelled at when I knew I was good at my job.

Stella probably wasn't too happy with me, but I couldn't work at a job where I was treated this way. We had children and I needed income. I knew something else would come up. It always did.

I used to help a lot of illegals fill out their paperwork, so they could be here legally. There was this one kid I helped who was a painter. He learned I was out of a job, so he came over to my house and told me, "Be ready. Tomorrow, I'll pick you up. You're going to be a painter."

# Jimmy the Greek

I started working with him on the New York City housing projects. He worked with me, side by side. I had to paint twelve rooms a week to keep the job. Since I was brand new, I was slow. I may have painted seven or eight. He helped me meet my quota. After a while, I was on my own. I was a painter.

I worked in the twin towers for eight months painting the elevator walls going all the way to the top of the building. When I was at the top, I could look down and see nothing. It was like being in an airplane. When the towers fell, my heart sunk. Not just because of the loss of life, which was horrible, but also because I had contributed just a small part in something so great which was no more. The buildings were a beautiful accomplishment. Something I was proud of. Terrorists destroyed a small piece of me that day when they destroyed the building I had helped create.

One building in New York City I helped paint was another piece of architectural beauty—St. Patrick's Cathedral. I heard so many masses I nearly became Catholic. The Irish Catholics love that church. When the building turned 100 the church members decided to renovate, which is how I ended up working in the beautiful church.

Stella worked in the garment district as a finisher. She used to stitch the lining inside the fur. She was really good at it. Both my brother and sister were still furriers and helped her get the job. She was a talented seamstress. Even after I married, we all still worked together to make ends meet. Life was getting better, but everything takes time.

When we bought the house in Queens, my parents lived with us. My father moved out after my mother died but he would still come and visit us. All the houses looked the same—row houses, they were called. Back then we never had to lock our doors, everyone just left them open and people would come and go as they pleased.

Next door to us lived an Irishman and his family. One snowy day my father came to visit. The only thing that was different about my house, from all the other houses on the street, was I had a crooked tree in my front yard. The snow made it hard to tell which tree was crooked, so he guessed which house was ours. He walked in the door, like everyone else did, and he looked around and asked, what happened? Did you redecorate?" The Irish family was all sitting there looking at him, wondering what he was doing. Thankfully they recognized him. He realized his mistake, apologized, then left and came to our house.

It was at that same house I had a German Shepherd. We called her Susie. She was the family dog, but really, she was my dog. She would spend her days outside in the yard, but at night, I would bring her in. She would lie outside the kids' bedroom and she wouldn't move a muscle all night long. She was their protector.

She had a litter of puppies and it was getting quite cold outside. Stella decided she better bring the puppies in to keep them warm. Susie didn't let her get close enough. She was growling at Stella. Come to find out, Stella wore my jacket outside to get the pups. Susie knew it wasn't me wearing my coat and she warned Stella to stay away.

If a stranger had come close, she would have done more than growl. Dogs are loyal creatures. They'll do anything for their family. I get that. Some people are that way too. When we moved to Texas, we took her with us.

Another job I held was as a stand-up delivery driver for Dugan's Bakery. Every morning I would deliver bread, cupcakes, and cakes door to door. We were part of the Local 802 Teamsters Union—bakery driver's union. The Dugan's bakery took up a whole city block and it was three stories high. It was the largest bakery of its kind in the United States. Some trucks had little bells on them and the driver would ring the bell to let people in the neighborhood know they were coming. People could shop from the back of the trucks. In other neighborhoods, customers would put a cardboard D in their window if they needed the driver to stop. These drivers went door to door with a tray of goods and the customers shopped from the trays. Our most popular items were the cupcakes and the crumb cake. People still rave about their baked goods.

The employee contract was up for renewal, so the union called a meeting. They said we should get a 100% raise. A raise sounded good. So, the employees agreed. We were all in a large barn. We called Mr. Clark, the owner of the company, to come in, and we told him we'd like a 100% raise. He told us, "You do deserve a raise, but not a 100% raise. I will give you a 50% raise.

The union said, no, we aren't going to agree to that. Mr. Clark told everyone, "If you don't agree to the 50% raise, I'll close the company."

The union assured us he was bluffing so we didn't agree. Mr. Clark didn't say a word. He went home. We all did the same. The next day we went to work and there were signs on the doors saying, "Closed." I had a good job with an owner who was fair, and the Union got greedy. They wanted that bump in Union dues. I lost a good job that day. I haven't been a fan of Unions since.

All winter long I worked 6 long days a week. Summer was a different story. For 2 months I took off Saturday and Sunday, so I could take my family to the beach. Stella would make a batch of spaghetti or stuffed cabbage and we'd leave early in the morning, before the morning work traffic, to make the 30-minute drive. We'd swim and fish, eat lunch, the kids would play on the swings then we'd leave for home by two or three o'clock in the afternoon, before evening traffic became really bad. Traffic in New York City has always been crazy.

Stella never did get her driver's license. Had we lived in the country, maybe I could have talked her into driving. But, living in a city, especially New York City, scared her to death. Big city driving combined with one bad memory, and she didn't want to drive ever again. Right after we were married, Stella and my sister took my car and drove it around the block. I had no idea they went for a joy ride (even if they didn't go more than 5 miles per hour). I just knew when I went to get my car, it was gone. I thought it was stolen. Maria was driving but Stella was there too. I was watching and here they came, down the block, driving like my grandmother might have driven. I might have gotten a little bit upset. After that experience, Stella didn't want anything to do with driving.

Jones Beach reminded me of Leros. It's an island with six and a half miles of white sand beaches on the Atlantic. Of course, it would remind me of Leros. These days, Jones Beach has restaurants, swimming pools, miniature golf, even a theater that seats fifteen thousand people. Really, a Hamptons for us regular people. I've always loved the sea and living in a big city took some adjusting. Having the ocean nearby helped. Listening to the waves beat against the sand gave my children a little bit of the home I remembered growing up in. Later, they would make the journey across the ocean to Leros. Jones Beach provided just a small taste until we could afford that trip.

# Chapter 15
# Family Life

*"What you leave behind is not what is engraved in stone monuments, but what is woven into the lives of others." Pericles, Stateman, Orator, and General from the 5$^{th}$ century BC*

With each generation, the yearning for the homeland grows less. My father, he missed Leros and went back a couple of times, the last time he stayed. He always defended Mussolini saying Mussolini did what he had to do to save Italy, more so Rome. If he hadn't of joined Hitler, then Hitler would have destroyed Italy. He would have bombed her churches and her historic buildings. He said Mussolini sacrificed himself to save his people. Many people disagree with that theory, but I tend to believe my father. I think Hitler gave Mussolini an ultimatum. I'm sure there is a lot that happened that we'll never know about. We moved on. We survived.

I believe my father was somewhat lost after we came back to Leros from the refugee camp. Someone had ratted him out. His business was gone. Our home was no longer ours. His standing on the island as a man of authority—someone to reckon with—was no more. Although he never stopped trying, after the war he had a hard time providing for our family. After being hugely successful, and then also being a guard in a large refugee camp with thousands of refugees, somewhere along the way he lost his confidence and his belief he was a man of influence. He'd always been an important man; a man who was successful and a man who people looked up to. After the war, that all changed. I don't think he ever got over what happened. It seemed he would move from one business idea to the next, trying to replace what was lost to him, yet never finding his place.

Even when my father returned to Leros the final time, he took large cases full of dresses with the goal of opening a store. When he arrived, all my female cousins, as well as other ladies, fell in love with the dresses so he ended up just giving them away. His heart was always bigger than his desire for money.

Instead of opening a store, he found a new wife and settled back down on Leros. They built a house together and that is where he lived the rest of his days. I believe he longed for Leros, he missed the life he used to lead. Sometimes I feel that longing but, after being an American for so many years, it is not easy to go back. When a person comes to know everything America has to offer, the value of a dollar, the availability of gasoline, the freedom to disagree with government, free speech, and all the other benefits of being an American, going back isn't really an option. It would be too hard to give up everything America offers.

I'd visited my father a time or two when he lived on Leros, but as you know, life gets busy and it's easy to get caught up in everyday life and the demands of having a family.

There are phone calls that are serious enough they change plans and make you visit, even when life is too busy. In 1978 I received one of those phone calls. My dad was having pancreatic surgery. I flew out of New York and headed to Leros. Family is everything.

The doctors removed his pancreas. He had cancer. I'd already lost my mom to cancer, now, I was losing my dad too. He took me for a walk on his beautiful island and said, "Jimmy, people think I'm stupid. They say to me, 'you won't die. Everything will be okay.' But, I know I'm dying. Everyone is trying to calm me down and give me peace but I'm not afraid to die. Whatever is going to happen, will happen."

I didn't know what to say. What could I say? He was right. How can we, mere mortals, change the future? We will all die. Maybe not today. Maybe not tomorrow. But, one day we will die.

He put his hand across my shoulders and said, "I'm glad you came to visit."

I reached in my pocket and pulled out the last $10 I owed him from loaning me money to go back to Leros to marry Stella. He was like an elephant. He didn't forget anything, especially when it came to money. Every time he saw me, he reminded me I still owed him $10. I'm pretty sure I paid it back already but who knows, he was the money man. What's another $10? Besides, he would have come back from the grave to get his money!

I represented our whole family. No one else was able to go. I went home and a few months later, he died. His second wife is still living. We visit her when we go back to Leros. She's living in a nursing home now.

My brother, Steve, was the most determined of all my brothers and sisters. He knew exactly what he wanted to be, and he didn't stop until he got what he wanted—he has his doctoral degree in engineering. He's retired now. He and his wife have three boys.

My sister Chrissy was the oldest, then Steve, John, me (Jimmy), Tony, Irene, and Maria, in that order. My mom miscarried several and my little brother died when we were in Palestine. If all her babies would have lived, there would have been about a dozen of us.

John and Chrissy were both Furriers. They started out in the garment district after we moved from Leros to New York City. John was a chain smoker, I mean, he'd light up one right after the other and use a tweezers to hold the butt to light the next cigarette. Ten packs a day. He stopped smoking 40 years ago. As much as he smoked, it was my brother, Tony, that ended up with lung cancer. It's weird how things work out. Not exactly like you'd expect them to. Tony lived in Seattle with his wife and they had a nightclub.

# Chapter 16
# Moving to Texas

*"There is nothing permanent except change."*
*Heraclitus, Philosopher of the 4th century BC*

I had lived in New York for thirty years. It was home. When my brother, Tony, was diagnosed with lung cancer, he traveled from Seattle, Washington to DM Anderson Cancer Center in Houston, Texas. He noticed how beautiful it was, and how the climate was similar to Leros. When he learned the economy was booming, he called me up and said, "Jimmy, you've gotta come down here and check it out." So, I did.

Tony had a nightclub and a restaurant in Seattle where he played with a band. His wife, son, and daughter are still living there. The cancer beat my brother. He didn't make it. We helped out after he passed, as much as we could.

When I arrived in Houston, I realized a good thing when I saw it. There was—there still is—business opportunities in Houston, so I moved my family down.

My wife, Stella, didn't really want to be there. My daughter, Sophia, hated it. My son, Peter, he did okay.

We lived in an apartment building to start with. Every day I would go check the mail and every day there was a note in our black mailbox which read, "Yankee, go home!" I wanted to hang a sign from my window saying, "I'm Greek! I'm not a Yankee!"

We lived in the apartment for about a year and a half then we bought the house we live in. It was brand new. The builders had just finished building it. We've been in Texas for 37 years. Sophia still wants to move back to New York. I have to admit, Houston is a lot different than New York City.

My brother, Steve, is the oldest boy and the smartest in our family. When we came to the USA, not long after, he was working and also going to night school to become an electrical engineer. He ended up getting his doctorate in Electrical Engineering. When the first rocket went to the moon, I believe he was involved with the project. He also was an adviser as a dancing teacher at a Greek and American organization.

Sophia was almost 16 and Peter was 11 when we moved from New York City to Houston. Sophia hated it. She didn't want to go. All her friends were in New York.

One night, Stella woke me up. "Jimmy, Sophia isn't home. It's 11 o'clock. Go find her. I'm worried." I didn't even take the time to get dressed. I drove to her work in my robe. She was so embarrassed. She worked in a jewelry store and they got to talking after work and the time passed fast. She wasn't doing anything bad. I don't get so worked up, but Stella, she worries.

Houston is home to me. This house is where my grandchildren, Soto and Alexandria, grew up. So many of our memories are here. This is where I want to live until I die.

After our daughter, Sophia, met Theo and married him, they lived with us. When they had our grandson, Soto, they were here still. Oh, he was such a difficult baby. He would cry, and Stella and I would help by staying up with him at night. We nearly wore a path in our floor walking with him. I think that might be why he is so close to our hearts. We were with him so much. He was about two years old when we bought a house just like ours five doors down. Sophia and Theo moved in there and my son, Peter, and his wife, lived with us still. My daughter, my son, my grandchildren, have always lived with us or close by. We've never lived far apart. That is important to me. I want my family close by. They are the most important part of my life.

My oldest sister, Chrissy, she was fun to be around. She was the furrier. When she got married she quit her job. She and her husband moved to Texas. Later, the furrier shops closed up. China started making everything much cheaper. A lot of people lost jobs. The quality of the products went down. Maybe now, that we're going to have a fairer trade act with China, maybe now some of those businesses will come back to the United States. Chrissy passed away in the early 2000's. My other sister, Maria, and her husband moved to Texas too. She was a hairdresser.

Today, Irene and Maria live together in California. Jeff, Irene's son-in-law, bought her a house so she could be near her grandchildren. They are very happy.

As I mentioned before, when I was younger I wanted to be a priest. After my mom died, that changed. I think in some ways, I was a little lost. Even though I was upset with God, in some ways the church was still important to me. I think because it had been such a big part of my life for so many years. It's hard to completely let go of something that important.

There was a Greek Orthodox priest who would come to the Texaco station that I owned. I asked him, "How come we can't build a church here?" The church we were going to was over 20 miles away. He said the secret is having a lot of families who want a church in one location. Once we find that many families, we can ask for a church. So, that is what we did. My brother-in-law and I found 35 families who wanted a church closer to where we lived. Now, we have a beautiful Greek Orthodox Church—a big one—St. Basil the Great Greek Orthodox Church. It cost about 15 million dollars and we got it going. That happened shortly before Stella and I went to San Antonio, so others took over when we left. But, we still had a hand in getting it started. The church is still going strong. We have a lot of festivals and I'm glad it's close by for Stella. Religion is very important to her.

# Chapter 17
# Texas: Building a Business

*"Make the best use of what's in your power and take the rest as it happens." Epictetus, Philosopher of the 1ˢᵗ century AD*

My desire to help others has never gone away. In fact, if I look back at how many people we've helped, who have gone on to be millionaires—and have never even come back to say thank you—I'd do it all over again. Maybe not everything, but certainly most everything. There are times I put my family second to help other people. I didn't mean to, I wouldn't choose to do that, but I did without thinking about it. When I see someone hurting—hungry and without the basics to survive—I remember what I went through and my heart just goes out to them. I help without thinking of what I might get in return, or how helping them will help me. I do it because I care about people.

After we moved to Texas I bought a Texaco, the business, not the building. I leased the building but bought the business. Texaco gives you four years to become successful, after that, you're on your own. I borrowed to buy the business and they accepted me as a Texaco dealer. The building was dilapidated and when I bought it, the station was only selling 20,000 gallons of gasoline. I got it up to 60,000. Everything was going really well. Texaco was looking after our business. They fixed up the building, almost like brand new, and they wanted to sell it but, because I borrowed to buy the business, I didn't have enough equity to borrow more for the building. They wanted half a million dollars. So, I ended up losing the business. After I went bankrupt, everyone would come up to me and ask me why I was so happy. I lost everything, I must be upset. I said, what do you want me to do? Sit down and cry? No, I just get up and keep moving forward. A trait I inherited from both my parents. You just keep going—keep putting one foot in front of the other and deal with what has to be dealt with.

Part of the reason I wasn't the greatest businessman was, if someone came and needed to have their car fixed so they could get to work, and they didn't have the money, I let them pay me later. Some would say, "Jimmy, I don't have my checkbook with me. Can I take my car and come back in and pay you tomorrow?" I'd say, "sure, go ahead." In a lot of those cases, I'm still waiting for them to come pay me.

When I was a young boy, I remember my parents helping refugees, many of them were illegal. Some jumped ship to swim to the shore. They came to our house and we helped them. My mother was feeding them, cleaning them up and giving them some clothes. That sort of thing. Many went on to become successful citizens. That I know of, none of them came back to say thank you. That's the way it is sometimes. People don't always remember who helped them along the way.

I owned another Texaco on the corner of Highway 6 and 110 here in Houston. There was a relative of mine, he had a small baby. Actually, the baby was his nephew. His sister was crazy—taking drugs or something. His name was George Palatianos. He was sleeping in the streets with a kid. I took him out of the street, I hired him, and he was working for me at night when the baby was sleeping. During the day he ended up finding a job and got an apartment. Well, his brother-in-law owned what is now J&T Automotive. The building, in the Spring Branch area, used to house a Firestone station. George called and let me know his brother-in-law was losing the business. He couldn't pay the bills. He told us if we could come up with ten thousand dollars, we could take over.

We went to the bank and we got the mortgage. At that time my son-in-law, Theo, was working for me as a mechanic at the Texaco. We managed to get the building and the business. We paid something like five thousand a month. My brother had a friend in Seattle who was a mechanic. He said the guy was a good mechanic but wasn't doing well in Seattle. This is when we made a deal with the devil.

# Jimmy the Greek

I brought the guy down from Seattle, Washington to help out with the business. He was working for Mercedes and barely making anything. He was making a thousand dollars a week in our business; a lot more than he was in Seattle. My son in law didn't speak that great of English, so having someone who spoke good English really helped. He ended up becoming partners with Theo, who was running the business. My son-in-law retained 51% control and his partner had the other 49%.

About that time, Theo started getting sick—he was in and out of the hospital. He took a third of his paycheck and gave it to his partner because his partner was running the place by himself. It wasn't really that bad, but he said he was tired and stressed out, so he went to court and pushed my son-in-law out of the business. He threw us out of our own business. There was nothing we could do. We didn't have the money to fight him. We were so busy and so tired taking care of Theo, we didn't have the energy. On top of everything else, we found out he was embezzling.

He began threatening me, sending letters with lies trying to make trouble for my family. He and his wife threatened me, and my family and I told him, if he ever did anything to hurt anyone I love, he better disappear from the face of the earth because I would track him down and make him pay. I won't stand by and let anyone hurt my family. Ever.

When they first came, we helped them. When I think of everything we did—my wife was babysitting their babies, my daughter was taking the children to school, they ate and drank at our home, we helped them find an apartment—I guess everything we did wasn't appreciated. I did my part. I know what we did. I guess that is all that matters, that I did the right thing. Sometimes though, it hurts when you know you've given so much and people just take advantage of you. They had kids. In the end, I had to do what was best for those kids.

I tried to get a loan to buy the business back, but even though our credit was good, the bank wouldn't give it to us. They said the ground was contaminated from a leaky storage container and they wouldn't loan anyone the money to buy the building.

I was out of money. I had to do something to survive. One of my customers was a painting contractor. He knew I had done some painting in New York City when I was younger, so he offered me a job painting a house.

He gave me all the instructions then gave me the key to the house. I was painting the house when this guy walks in the door. I was mad, cursing—in Greek. I said, "Sir, where are you going?"

He said, "This is my house."

I replied, "I don't know you. While I'm here, I'm responsible for this house."

He said, "Don't worry. This is my house." Then he told me the name of the guy who hired me. Once he gave me enough information, I knew he was okay. He went in and did some stuff then he came back out to me and said, "I heard you cursing. What language was that?"

I told him Greek and he wanted to know why I was cursing. So, I told him the story of what was happening with our business and the embezzling, and how I took this job just to make ends meet. We need three hundred and fifty thousand dollars to buy the guy out and our bank won't give us the money.

He told me to bring him the paperwork. I told him I'd bring it the next morning when I came into work and he said, "No, put the paint brush down and go get the paperwork now."

Three days later we had a check for three hundred and fifty thousand dollars. That is a miracle. Turns out he was the president of Citizen's Bank which is now Prosperity Bank. We are still doing business with them today.

After we got the money to buy our business back, Theo wanted to go to the shop. It was Sunday and the next day we were supposed to sign the papers. I tried to talk him out of going to the shop, but for some reason, Theo really wanted to go, so I took him.

We had a locksmith meet us there and open the place for us. Theo wanted Peter to bring his tools in and get ready for work. Well, Dimitrious—his name is the same as my Greek name—found out and came through the door with a sledgehammer. I had my back to him and he grabbed me and was about to hit me with the hammer when his wife ran in and stopped him. He would have killed me.

We shouldn't have gone to the shop. I know that. We had one more day and then it would be ours. We could have waited.

When Theo died, this guy, Dimitrious, who was supposed to be a good friend, didn't come to his funeral.

He wasn't really a friend. He used us to get where he is today. That's all we were to him. People to walk on.

We got our business back and we didn't press charges because the guy had a wife and kids. I still had compassion for him even though he didn't deserve it. He's still around but I don't want anything to do with him.

I wanted to expand our business, so I bought two gas stations in San Antonio. Stella and I moved into an apartment there while I worked on building the business. After a year and a half, I decided they just weren't making any money. We missed our family. We missed our home. So, I sold them, and I didn't tell Stella what I was doing until it was done.

One day I came home and told her to pack, we're going home. She asked, "What about the gas stations?"

I said, "No more. We're going home." When we traveled back and forth between Houston and San Antonio, we would pass this big outdoor décor place. They sold big pots, and animals—stuff made out of cement to decorate the yard with. Every time we passed by Stella would want to stop in and buy something, but we didn't have the money. As we were driving home that final time, I pulled into the parking lot and said, "Pick out whatever you want!"

That little deer she bought—it looks like a donkey—is still sitting in our front yard.

Today, my daughter, Sophia, and my grandson, Soto, are the bosses—not me. I'm just the "go get it" man. I pick up parts. I drive people home. I pick them up, so they can get their cars. I get lunch. I do whatever they need me to do. In 2005 Theo died...and Sophia used the insurance money to make sure no one ever took the business away from our family again.

# Chapter 18
# Being Greek in Texas

*"The most difficult thing in life is to know yourself." – Thales, Greek Philosopher of the 5th century BC*

When we first moved to Texas we had a small Greek community. We enjoyed a meal together. We'd celebrate together. Raise a toast when the occasion came up. There were still some Greek weddings to play for, some Greeks who loved their culture and wanted to keep traditions alive. I thought I would be as busy in Houston as I was in New York, but that wasn't the case. I have played for maybe three Greek weddings in 37 years.

Today, those same people, the people who are my age, are dying and their kids want to be American. They've given up keeping our culture alive. I believe I can be both, American and Greek.

In New York City, the Greek traditions are still strong, maybe not like they used to be, but still going. Here in Texas, not so much. The younger people forget they're

Greek. We need more immigrants who know what it means to be American. I just wish they wouldn't forget where they come from. There is so much to be learned from the past.

If you have seen the movie, My Big Fat Greek Wedding, you probably remember Windex being used to cure everything from acne to poison ivy to mosquito bites. Well, the funny thing is, every family has a different cure all. In our family, it's rubbing alcohol. We use it on everything. If you get a scratch or have a rash, you better run. Stella will be coming for you and that stuff burns!

Another belief you will see from local Greeks is, they put a little gold pin, with a blue eye (in Greek: to kako mati) on a baby to keep the evil spirits or curses away. You may see this on the back of their clothing where they can't accidently take it off and hurt themselves.

We are a very superstitious people who are steeped in tradition. The two I mentioned above are just examples and I could tell you about many more. I could fill another book, probably many books, with just our customs and beliefs.

In New York City, being Greek or Irish or Italian still means something. Every year the Irish have a parade. They don't care if it rains or snows, they still have the parade. They want to have fun and celebrate their heritage. I think kids are missing that dedication today, the idea they came from someplace else.

If you want to learn more about being Greek in Houston, you should attend one of the Greek Festivals in the area. You'll experience authentic Greek food, tours of the church, live music, dancing, shopping, and of course, drinking. We have one in May at our church, St. Basil the Great Greek Orthodox Church. There is another one in October at another church. It's a great way to experience being Greek in Texas and connecting with others of the same heritage. And if you aren't Greek, come on over anyway. We love to share our heritage with anyone and everyone!

In order to keep playing the music I love, I play at a Greek restaurant named Simply Greek every Saturday night. We have a band, a belly dancer, and wonderful Greek food. The interesting thing is, most of the people coming to eat aren't Greek. They just enjoy the entertainment and the food. We have a lot of fun and I look forward to playing. Sometimes, we all stand in a line and dance out the door of the restaurant making a large loop then back in again. The people love it! So do I. It's one way I keep the Greek traditions alive in me and remember where I came from.

Growing up poor has always given me a desire to help others. I think back to my reaction to the guy wasting crackers in the Navy. Or the Greek soldiers eating poorly while American soldiers were eating like kings. Even though I'm against government handouts, that doesn't mean I think we shouldn't help those who don't have enough food or shelter. And even though there have been many people my family and I have helped over the years who haven't stopped to say thank you, or what can I help you with, I would do everything I've done to help others all over again. I may get disappointed. I might be hurt. But I'd help them all again.

Well, there's just one guy who I wouldn't help again. You know who that is. The guy who tossed us out of our business when my son in law was sick. I've never hated anyone—accept him. I can say I hated him. He hurt my family. And what did I say about understanding a dog's loyalty to his family? I am too and when he hurt my family, he hurt me.

When I was younger, and I worked in New York, a lot of the time I worked for cash. Because of this, my social security payments are very low. I got to thinking about immigrants today and all the illegal immigration going on. I worked in this city for 37 years. Before that, I worked in New York City for 30 years. That is 67 years working in America—and maybe I can borrow President Trump's slogan—to Make America Great (Again). I'm 80 years old and I'm blessed because I have family here who makes sure I'm taken care of. But I decided to conduct an experiment.

I went to the welfare office and I applied for food stamps. I wouldn't have taken them, but I wanted to see what would happen, what they would say. I applied, and I waited. Finally, I heard back from them. I qualified for food stamps, but I couldn't get them. I asked, "if I qualify, why can't I get them?"

The lady at the office looked at me and said, "Well, you can get them if you sell your house. You can't own your house and get help." I was so angry. We have people coming here illegally every single day and they get help from our government. They get food, they get housing, they get all kinds of stuff. But, because I worked hard and saved and sacrificed so I could buy a home, I can get no help. Something is wrong in our state, in our country, if the government wants to reward people who have no goals and refuse to work.

# Chapter 19

# I'm American but I'll always be Greek

*"Neither by nature, then, nor contrary to nature do the virtues arise in us; rather we are adapted by nature to receive them, and are made perfect by habit" – Aristotle, Philosopher of the 4$^{th}$ century BC*

I've been an American for 67 years. I've been Greek for 80 years. The math doesn't add up, but that's the way it works sometimes.

For four hundred years Leros was passed around from country to country, the most recent being Turkey and

Italy. Yet, somehow, we were always Greek. We always identified as being Greek. My grandfather was a Turkish police chief—yet he was Greek. My mother made spaghetti—yet she was Greek. My father was a powerful man in our community—similar to the Italian hierarchy—yet he was Greek. Greek is in our blood. It's who we are.

I look at Greece today and think, maybe the Italians should have kept Leros. The Island would be in better shape. Even if they had, we'd still be Greek. In Greece we have 8 major parties, over 50 minor parties and 300 members of parliament representing just under 11 million people. Let me put this in perspective. The UK has 650 members of parliament representing just over 65 million people. You do the math. And the Greek politicians make more than the UK's members of parliament. The money paid out to these professional politicians do nothing for the people.

The average Greek makes 1092 Euros, or just over $1200 dollars per month. On a tourist destination like Leros, $1200 doesn't take you too far.

June through September the average number of rainy days is zero and the daily temperatures range from 76 degrees to 90 degrees. Certainly, hot enough to swim in the ocean. Yet, step under a shade tree and you have instant relief. Not bad for paradise. So, for four months straight, tourists visit Leros, swim the ocean, have picnics on beaches, climb the mountains, and basically just enjoy the rich culture and the hospitality of the Greeks without any chance for bad weather. For four months tourists pour funds into the local economy, so the Greeks can survive. One thing is for sure, the locals may not have much money, but they will feed you until you pop. And you can bet the food will be delicious!

August 15 is Santa Maria, a public holiday when we celebrate the mother of Jesus. The whole island is one big party. No one wants to sleep. Everyone is eating, drinking, dancing and having a good time. August 15 also marks the beginning of the end of tourist season. The weather will start getting a little cooler and the money will stop flowing quite as freely. Most Greeks hunker down for the winter, rarely turning on the electric heaters because electricity is so expensive. Most have little stoves they use to warm up their stone or cement houses.

The water in Leros isn't so good. People collect rain water during the fall, winter, and spring. It does not rain in the summer, so they use the water they have collected for the summer months. The city also removes salt from the sea water and the people use that. It still has a salty taste to it. I don't like it, so I bought a purifier for our home on Leros. And I use a bottle of purified water for a quick rinse after I finish showering. My skin still has a salty feel to it when I only use the island water to shower. The island has started getting machines from Europe to help them do a better job of purifying their water. Some of the other islands—the ones with more tourists—have better water supplies. I think as Leros grows into a more popular tourist destination, everything will improve.

I visited Leros the summer of 2017. My daughter used her airline points and gave Stella and I first class tickets to fly. We had so much room. We were so comfortable. We had a little champagne. A little wine. Stella's back is bad, it's hard for her to sit for a long period of time. The seats recline so you can lay back. First class was much easier on Stella for traveling. If you've never flown first class, you have to do it at least once in your life. Trust me. You'll never want to fly coach again.

When you are from Leros, and you're traveling back to Leros, make sure you take gifts. You must have gifts. Even if you are a visitor, if someone invited you to their home, take them flowers, or candy, or wine…take them something. It is good manners in Greece to give gifts. At our age I think it would be easier to just take a roll of money and give everyone a little cash. It would certainly be easier to carry rather than all the bulky presents.

After we arrive, our family and friends start showing up to see us—to welcome us home. Stella likes to have a present ready for each person who comes. I think we should act like the tourists and leave in the morning and go sightseeing all day, but she won't' let me. She loves to sit and relax and stare at the sea.

While we were there, I paid 60 euros for two pizzas. The people on Leros can't afford that. Only the tourists can eat pizza from the pizza shops. The people are taxed to death. Houses on Leros were passed down from generation to generation. Now, the young people don't want their family houses because the government started taxing home owners. They cannot afford to pay the taxes. Maybe that is what the government wants, to own all the land? I do not know but the people suffer. It breaks my heart to see my childhood home this way.

# Jimmy the Greek

I own a house on Leros. I inherited the house my father and stepmother built. It's not that big but it's comfortable. We have air conditioning. It sits on a hill and the sea views are gorgeous. Across the street is a small beach that isn't very busy. You can go swimming any time you want to.

My sister-in-law inherited the house on the hill where Stella lived before we got married—the one 365 steps from a castle with a church in it—which is convenient because Koula gets up every morning when we are there and climbs the steps to go to church. We often travel together and between the two houses, we have room to stay. Soto and I slept on the floor the last time we went. There weren't enough beds. Best sleep I've had in a while.

During the war, the walls of the castle used to hold the German spotlights as well as cannons. Guards were placed all around. You could see far from that height and the Germans took advantage of the location. In fact, for as long as people have been fighting over Leros, the mountain top has been used strategically to maintain control of the island.

Today the mountain top is highly protected. A person can only go so far in exploring. Who knows what they are hiding? An atomic bomb? Maybe, maybe not. But they are very secretive. When we visited Leros, Soto and I went to the mountain top and for some reason, they allowed us to enter the grounds. We couldn't go inside, but we were able to walk around and explore some. There were many small rooms. It is obvious Turkey wants to take the island again.

The mountain top is still being used to protect and maintain control of Leros.

I cannot imagine how the builders managed to get the stone up that mountain to build the castle. You would be amazed. Nearly every Greek island has a castle on a mountain top, so the islanders could protect themselves. I believe our work ethic was passed down from those before us who knew what hard work really was.

I think part of the reason I love Texas is the climate reminds me of Leros. Yes, I miss having a rich Greek community, but in Texas, there are years I have to turn on my air conditioning at Christmas time. I could do that in New York City, simply by opening my window!

Even in January and February, you're likely to see temperatures in the upper forties or lower fifties. A light jacket and you can roam the island without the crowds of summer. It might be a little chilly to swim though.

Today, in Leros, times have changed. As with most societies, the old ways get replaced with the new. The square is now open to anyone. Wives no longer get beat for walking through the square. There are bakeries and coffee shops with tables and chairs outside. There are cafes—where you can get the best gyros—and souvenir shops. People gather, women too, to talk and gossip and just enjoy the warm weather.

When I was a painter, I hated painting the projects. I watched so many people being handed brand new apartments and they didn't care about them, they didn't take any pride in what they were given. When someone has to work for something, they take pride in it. They work hard and know how much that thing cost. When a person is given money, or food, or clothing, or housing, they only know they got it for free and they come to expect everything to be free. I watched these people go up to the mailman and say, "Where is my check?" Lazy people don't work for what they need.

The government wants people to be dependent upon them. Politicians keep giving free stuff, so people will vote for them. It's much worse today. Everyone wants a handout. Now, the refugees are also getting handouts. When we came to America, we didn't expect anything to be free. We knew it was going to be hard work. We were going to have be patient. Now, everyone walks around with their hands out.

Today, we criticize what is happening in America. I can tell you this, you do not know how good you have it until you live somewhere else. If you want to burn the flag, go live in Greece. Go live in China or North Korea. See what happens when you burn those flags. Go live anywhere you think you might have more freedom, and more opportunity. No other country is like America. Not even the good ones measure up.

For instance, in Leros, you can be thrown in jail if you are accused of stealing or injuring someone, even if there is no proof, you can be put in jail. In America, you have rights. You have due process. There is democracy. One example: In Greece if you are suspected of being HIV positive, you can be detained and forced to take a test to determine if you truly are HIV positive. A landlord can evict you if you're tested positive. In the United States, you may face discrimination if you're suspected of being HIV positive, but you won't have mandatory testing, nor will you legally be evicted because of your disease.

Even with all the problems in Leros and Greek politics, I still say my island is the most beautiful island. A person can visit Lakki and eat a steak that melts in your mouth—or eat fresh seafood while watching the birds dive for their supper. You can watch the sun rise over the sea then turn around and watch it set over the sea. There are other islands you can visit, but Leros is the best.

# Chapter 20
# Coming to Terms with Aging

*"It is possible to provide security against other ills, but as far as death is concerned, we men live in a city without walls."* – Epicurus, Philosopher of the 4th century BC

There is one thing Stella and I disagree on, who gets to die first. Stella says she's already experienced so much heartache and loss and she can't take any more. So, she wants to be the first to go. I say, we should go together. I think she's okay with that, if that isn't the case, she definitely wants to be the first to go. She says it's her last wish and she always gets what she wishes for and she could not survive without me. We've been married for 55 years. Not that either of us are in any hurry to die, but, it's going to happen eventually.

My father didn't tell us kids anything. Today, I make sure my son knows I have a little money in this bank account in case we ever need it. I have some life insurance with such and such a company. It's best he knows these things, so he knows what to do when I die. We didn't know anything when my father died. I'm sure he had some cash stashed away, a little savings, but, we were never told.

I do want us to be able to die without being a burden to our children. We still have to decide what we're going to do with all the stuff we have stored in the garage. If we don't figure it out, they will have to and well, that's a lot of extra work for them. It's not like we use the stuff. I tell Stella, "We could be on that Hoarder's show. We have loads of stuff we haven't touched in years." I don't know what to do. Maybe we'll come to a decision one of these days. Lately she's been talking about getting rid of stuff more. I'm crossing my fingers.

But, I understand. Some things are more sentimental for Stella and harder to get rid of. I'd like to use the garage space to build a shower out there and maybe an extra bedroom. Stella? Not so much. Okay, so maybe we disagree on more than one thing. That's okay. It happens.

When I look back at my life, and I think about everything I've learned and everything I've done, I believe my proudest moment is going into the US Navy and serving my country. I was so thankful to be in America, serving made sense. Even before I was an American Citizen.

I believe more of our youth should serve in the military. I think our government should bring back the draft. In Israel, as soon as you are old enough, boy or girl, a gun is put your hands and you're taught to defend your nation. In the United States, these days, we are lacking pride. We have people burning the flag and stomping on it. We have people tearing down monuments and changing history simply because they do not like what happened in the past. They don't understand we need reminders from our past, so we remember the mistakes we made. Seeing the lack of values in our youth, that might be one of the hardest things I'm facing as I'm growing older.

I'm still against war. But, war will never end. People and governments will always be greedy and want more. They will always fight one another to take what isn't theirs. With 7 billion people on this earth, we will always have greedy power-hungry people. It's the way the world is.

I'm so proud of my children and grandchildren. Soto, he is our first grandchild and only grandson. He's our angel—our pride and joy. Our only granddaughter, Alexandra, she is beautiful. I want them both to understand their heritage, where they came from. Soto is learning to speak Greek a little better but Alexandra, not yet. She understands everything I say, but her lips won't move. She wouldn't say a word to anyone when we last visited Leros. Everyone thought she was mute. Hopefully one day she will be interested. My hope is before I die, they will know how important our family history is.

My daughter, Sophia, she loves Leros. Soto has begun to fall in love with the island too. The sunsets and sunrises, you've never seen anything like them. It is a beautiful land.

I come from a beautiful place. I want my grandchildren and great grandchildren to know where they come from.

I still have a few goals. Writing this book is one of them. I also want to make a difference, so I wrote President Trump. I told him what I thought about the draft and I gave him some good advice about health care. I don't know if he'll take my advice, but I got a letter back saying they were considering what I said. Who knows, maybe they take my advice and I save our health care system. Okay, probably not, but no one can say I didn't try.

I don't want to stop caring, to stop trying to make this world a better place. My grandchildren are grown up and someday they will have children of their own. What will this world look like for them? It's my job to care, to try to make things better until I breathe my last breath. And hopefully I've taught my children to care and take over where I left off.

When someone comes to America from Leros, they have probably been through hell. Say my nephew, he owned a grocery store and he lost his shirt. People are supposed to pay him, but they don't. He doesn't have any money. He comes here and all he sees are buildings, cars, stores, people everywhere…wealth everywhere. He works hard, and he builds a life for him and his family. His children remember the struggle, they remember the hard times from their younger years but his grandchildren, well, they don't remember the hard times so much because all the family has worked hard, and life has gotten better. Christmas presents are stacked all over the room—very different than receiving a penny as a child to buy some candy with and being overjoyed with the gift. I guess what I want for the generations that come after me is they're always thankful and proud to be an American. And at the same time, they're proud of being Greek.

When I was young, and we lived in New York City, if the subway ride went up a penny—from five cents to six cents—you should have heard the squawking. Everyone complained. Today? The price could rise to $14.00 for the subway in New York City and no one would say a word. They would just pay it. You park in Houston and the cost goes up a quarter, no one says anything. They just put another quarter in the little machine by the parking place and go about their business. No one complains. No one puts up a fight.

I think the passion is just gone. No one thinks they can make a difference, that they're somehow fighting all alone by themselves, that they're powerless.

I've been thinking about the world, and whether anything is better than when I was young. I know, I sound old. But, is anything better? We have people with their hands out expecting the government to take care of them. We have people who are trying to change everything this country stands for. Young people don't want to work or take pride in their country. There are still good people in this country, people who still care about what happens here. Even so, the fact remains there are less good people. There's more war. People hate each other. They're greedy and selfish. Everyone has their nose in a computer or their phones. People don't know how to have real relationships.

Things are more complicated. And more complicated doesn't necessarily mean better.

I would like to see a better world, but I don't think we're going to. We have peace right now, but I don't think we will for long. For now, it's enough. We have to keep trying to make a difference and change things for the better.

If there is one thing I regret, it would be not getting a better education. My brother Steve and I would jump out of bed every morning. We were so excited for school. All my other brothers and sisters—my mom had to drag them out of bed to get ready. They didn't want anything to do with school. I loved to learn. Knowledge is so important. I quit school when I was 15 and I never went back. And I loved school. But, when given the choice between eating and learning, a person will choose eating every time. You have to eat to be able to survive. I thought I could go back to school later. But, I never did.

I have been learning ever since, although not through going back to school. I read the newspaper and all through the Navy I was constantly learning. I may not be eloquently spoken since English is my second language, but as my friend Darlene said, I am intelligent, and I have a working knowledge of the English language. Even that is too many words for me. I'll put it simply—the way I say it is, I can make myself understood and I'm aware of what is happening around me. A bunch of fancy words don't make a person smart. It just proves he has read and memorized the dictionary. Even politicians can read words off a screen. Love to learn and you won't learn to impress others, you'll learn to better your own self. I will never stop learning. I'll keep learning until the day I die.

When I was thinking about what I fear most in life, I wasn't considering the state of the world for my grandchildren and great grandchildren. That puts fear in a whole different category.

If I could send a message to my grandchildren, great grandchildren, and to everyone who comes after me, I'd say, always love one another. Keep dreaming and growing. Keep learning. Be honest and be true, to yourselves, to others, and to your past as well as your future. Fight for what is right and never stop believing in yourself and what you can do. Respect others, even your enemies. When you decide to do something, just do it. Don't mess around. Don't use the word "try." Get rid of the word. You either do it or you don't. I say go into this world and make a difference. Be someone the world looks up to…and respects. You live in the greatest nation in the world, The United States of America. You have so much to be thankful for. Lastly, know that I love you.

There have been very few times I have cried in my life. Wisdom has opened my eyes enough to allow the tears to come through. When I was younger, not fulling understanding and pride kept my eyes shut tight. Now, I know. Life is short.

When my mother died, I cried a few tears, but I was more mad and my emotions came through as anger…toward life and toward God. Why does it take living a full life to fully understand what is important? I don't even claim to know the answer to that yet myself, but I'm getting there.

When my Godchild died the summer of 2016, I think I truly wept for the very first time. She came to New York City to have an operation. She had cancer. She made it through the operation, but she didn't live long afterward. I have cried tears in the past, but her death hit me hard. She was like a daughter to me. I realized how fragile life was and how quickly someone we love could just be gone, just like that. I thought of my children, of Soto and of Alexandria, and my heart twisted inside me. I felt real pain, not just emotional pain, and I wept great tears of sorrow.

The older we get, the less we take life for granted and instead we start cherishing life. As we grow old, when someone we love dies, we realize that soon, that will be us. We won't live forever, and we know that's how we're going to end up.

I don't plan on dying anytime soon! I'm in the best shape. I'm always moving, always on the go. I lost some weight eating low carb and my energy is just great. Since I'm a veteran, I have great health care through the VA. I do not understand all the complaining about veterans not getting health care. I receive the best care. I think people who like to complain will complain no matter what.

My doctor gives me a hug, she asks me if I need anything at all and tells me to call if anything comes up. I go in every year and if I don't do what I'm supposed to, she'll call my wife.

When I do die, I want a party—a big party. There is a gypsy tribe in Rajasthan, India—specifically the Satiyaa community—that mourns when a baby is born. They consider birth to be a punishment by God. Life is hard and full of disappointments. Living is much harder than dying. In the US, we celebrate birth. In Rajasthan, the family is not even allowed to cook with the rest of the tribe as a punishment for having a child. Instead of blessings or prayers, they curse the baby.

Death, however, is celebrated. As soon as the funeral pyre is lit, the feasting begins. They throw a party. They put on clean clothes. They buy sweets and dried fruit and have plenty of alcohol. Death of a family member is one of the happiest events in their lifetimes. They cremate the bodies and dance to the beat of pounding drums until the last of the body is turned to ash.

That is what I want—a party. I want everyone to celebrate my life and everything I've accomplished and everyone I've left behind. I don't want the Greek tradition of wailing, crying, and pulling hair. I want people to laugh and have fun, to tell jokes and eat my favorite foods. Someone better make cabbage rolls and Pastitsio then raise a glass of ouzo in a toast.

I know I'll be missed. And that's okay. But, we all have to die sometime. When I went to visit my aunt in Leros, I saw she was in constant pain. She was in bed for four years. No relief. She couldn't move. She was all alone. She would call me three times a week because she was lonely. She would ask me if I could give her some poison, so she could just die already. Death for many means an end to their agony. When I think back to my mother dying and how terrible I felt, now, I understand a little better. She was sick. She was in constant pain. I wouldn't have wanted my mother to lie in agony and keep living just because I would miss her when she was gone. That would be selfish of me. If God wasn't going to heal her, then it was better he took her quickly. I'm glad she didn't suffer for too long. A little piece of me still holds onto the faith of my childhood. The church was a big part of my life. I'm still looking for God to prove himself to me though. He needs to come through the door and kick the shit out of me, so I know it's him, that he is real.

I leave you knowing one more thing on my bucket list is complete. This book is written. This book holds my heart. It makes me glad knowing a piece of me will go on living, even when my body is gone.

Jimmy (Dimitrious) Proios